GW01454252

T H E Ull

WHERE THE WORLD MEETS TO PRAY

Sarah Wilke

Publisher

INTERDENOMINATIONAL

INTERNATIONAL

INTERRACIAL

33 LANGUAGES

Multiple formats are available in some languages

The Upper Room
September–December 2015
Edited by Susan Hibbins

The Upper Room © BRF 2015
The Bible Reading Fellowship
15 The Chambers, Vineyard, Abingdon OX14 3FE
Tel: 01865 319700; Fax: 01865 319701
Email: enquiries@brf.org.uk
Website: www.brf.org.uk
BRF is a Registered Charity

ISBN 978 0 85746 136 0

Acknowledgments

Printed by Gutenberg Press, Tarxien, Malta

The Upper Room is ideal in helping us spend a quiet time with God each day. Each daily entry is based on a passage of scripture, and is followed by a meditation and prayer. Each person who contributes a meditation to the magazine seeks to relate their experience of God in a way that will help those who use *The Upper Room* every day.

Here are some guidelines to help you make best use of *The Upper Room*:

1. Read the passage of Scripture. It is a good idea to read it more than once, in order to have a fuller understanding of what it is about and what you can learn from it.
2. Read the meditation. How does it relate to your own experience? Can you identify with what the writer has outlined from their own experience or understanding?
3. Pray the written prayer. Think about how you can use it to relate to people you know, or situations that need your prayers today.
4. Think about the contributor who has written the meditation. Some *Upper Room* users include this person in their prayers for the day.
5. Meditate on the 'Thought for the Day' and the 'Prayer Focus', perhaps using them again as the focus for prayer or direction for action.

Why is it important to have a daily quiet time? Many people will agree that it is the best way of keeping in touch every day with the God who sustains us, and who sends us out to do his will and show his love to the people we encounter each day. Meeting with God in this way reassures us of his presence with us, helps us to discern his will for us and makes us part of his worldwide family of Christian people through our prayers.

I hope that you will be encouraged as you use the magazine regularly as part of your daily devotions, and that God will richly bless you as you read his word and seek to learn more about him.

Susan Hibbins
UK Editor

In Times of/For Help with . . .

Below is a list of entries in this copy of *The Upper Room* relating to situations or emotions with which we may need help:

God's Grace Unbounded

'By grace you have been saved through faith, and this is not your own doing; it is the gift of God—not the result of works, so that no one may boast' (Ephesians 2:8–9).

'There but for the grace of God go I.'* This is an expression I often hear repeated when news of a tragedy breaks. We reach for it to cope with what can't be explained. We all want to know: if crime, accident or illness can happen to any of us, why did this happen to that person and not to me?

We lean on this expression for comfort or perhaps even to connect us to the suffering. But some years ago I gained a different perspective about this familiar saying from a woman who had survived a brutal, random kidnapping. In the aftermath, as she received consolation from family and friends, she quickly grew weary of hearing some people try to relate to her by invoking 'There but for the grace of God go I.'

She made me realise that an expression intended to comfort also carries with it something quite discomforting: the suggestion that anyone suffering tragedy has somehow slipped outside the bounds of God's grace.

The grace of God isn't a magic wand, waved to create danger-free zones for a lucky few. As Paul's letter to the Ephesians tells us, God's grace is a blessing extended to all. We don't have to do anything to earn it. And we certainly don't have to fear ever losing it. Just as God did not cause this woman's darkest hour so did he never abandon her throughout her ordeal.

I am thankful that I worship a God who extends grace to everyone, no matter what our fortunes or misfortunes are.

Indeed, the grace of God goes with us all.

Sarah Wilke, Publisher

*Attributed to John Bradford (1510–1555), English reformer and martyr.

The Upper Room contacted me in the early 1970s, proposing a partnership with New Day Publishers to begin producing an English-language edition of the daily devotional guide in the Philippines. Today, our Philippines-English edition has more than 2000 readers.

In 2009, Typhoon Ondov struck the Philippines and flooded our office. We were in very bad shape. We lost property and valuable files, including new books freshly delivered from the press. We had no electricity for almost a month, and we had to clean up the mud and damage in the darkness. Hearing of our situation, a devoted reader of The Upper Room came to our office. This reader showed compassion, telling us how much the devotional magazine had benefited her family. 'I grew up with The Upper Room,' she said, and she wanted to express her gratitude by doing something for us. She gave us a new computer and continues to be one of our most loyal readers.

As New Day is a typhoon survivor, I am a cancer survivor. In 2012, I was diagnosed with breast cancer. I underwent a mastectomy and seven cycles of chemotherapy. I continued to manage the publishing house, and God was faithful. Every day, through stories of other believers in The Upper Room, God reassured me with promises of hope, courage and guidance.

Please pray that the board of New Day will discern a fresh vision for its ministry, and that we will find ways to face new challenges. Also pray for our staff to continue our work with dedication and commitment.

Bezalie Bautista Uc-Kung
Editor of the Philippines-English edition of The Upper Room

The Editor writes...

I have a good friend with whom I meet from time to time. Over the years we have come to share our thoughts and insights into scripture, and we talk about what God is doing in our lives.

One day my friend rang me on the off chance that I was free to meet up in a couple of days' time, which I was. I was glad to see her as we hadn't met for several months. On a beautiful autumn day we sat outside in a place of beauty and peace, and she explained that she wanted to share a problem with me. I listened quietly while she opened her heart and we talked of what God was doing and would do to help in her situation. Then, I also talked about an issue that had been troubling me, and she in turn was able to offer advice and comfort.

With thankfulness in our hearts, we knew that the Holy Spirit had brought us together on that particular morning so that we could help each other. We both felt better for sharing our concerns, for remembering how God had helped us in the past and that his presence was with us there and then.

Later I reflected on how great God's care is for each of us, and how humbling it is to know that. It is not only in the crisis moments of our lives that God is with us; his concern reaches down to the everyday troubling problems we all have. Jesus' promise that 'the very hairs of your head are all numbered' (Luke 12:7, NIV) shows us that every part of who we are and what we do matters to God. And he knows just who to bring into our lives that we might help and support each other when the going gets tough.

Susan Hibbins
Editor of the UK edition

The Bible readings are selected with great care, and we urge you to include the suggested reading in your devotional time.

Chosen

Read Ephesians 1:3–14

God chose us in Christ to be holy and blameless in God's presence before the creation of the world.
Ephesians 1:4 (CEB)

I wasn't brought up to go to church. My family didn't discuss God, but my mother sang hymns as she went about her chores. As I listened to her sing, 'He walks with me, and he talks with me' and 'Precious Lord, take my hand', I began to know a heavenly Father who loved me. I began to talk to God daily and to pray when I was afraid or needed help. When I was in my twenties, I knelt in front of the TV during a Billy Graham crusade and gave my life to Christ.

In a household in which five children grew up without the benefit of Sunday school or conversations about God, our heavenly Father was made known to us. How much the Lord wants a relationship with us! God pursues us in many ways—in church, yes, and sometimes through television and music. The Lord is patient with us. He gives us every opportunity to respond to the call of faith.

Prayer: *Faithful God, thank you for knowing us, loving us, and pursuing us long before we recognise our need for you. Amen*

Thought for the day: God's love is made known to us in a variety of ways.

Diana L. Walters (Tennessee, US)

PRAYER FOCUS: THOSE WHO WORSHIP THROUGH MUSIC

Others First

Read Philippians 2:1–4
Let each of you look not to your own interests, but to the interests of others.
Philippians 2:4 (NRSV)

Recently while strolling home from work, I encountered one of my friends. As I saw her coming, I felt compelled to offer her a business suit of mine that I had been meaning to give away. When I told her about it, she replied that she had been jobless for a while, that the next day she was scheduled for the last in a series of job interviews, and that she needed a suit for the interview.

I could brush this off as a coincidence. But I strongly believe that God used me in that moment as an answer to this sister's immediate need. God relies on us to touch the lives of others and be a blessing to them.

When we are sensitive to the promptings of the Holy Spirit who dwells in us and are willing to be used by God, we can respond positively and with love to those around us. Our help need not be a big gesture or gift of something material. A warm smile, a comforting touch, a hug or an encouraging word can meet a person's immediate need by strengthening his or her will to persevere.

Prayer: *Dear Lord, help us to be aware of opportunities to be an answer to other people's prayers. In Jesus' name. Amen*

Thought for the day: Today I will be willing and ready to be used by God to help others.

Veronica Kamidi (Nairobi, Kenya)

Shaken

Read Isaiah 40:4–5

Every valley shall be filled, and every mountain and hill shall be made low, and the crooked shall be made straight, and the rough ways made smooth; and all flesh shall see the salvation of God.
Luke 3:5–6 (NRSV)

The shaking woke us. First a lurch, then a shift—our house and all within began to sway in the powerful earthquake. When it stopped, we waited with the rest of the city for the radio announcer's comforting words, 'All is well. The worst is over.' We didn't stop to wonder why there had been an earthquake, because we knew that living in California meant that we would experience earthquakes once in a while.

Around the same time, our family suffered a devastating job loss that shook our sense of security. And this time, no announcer was there to tell us the worst was over. All we could do was to hang on to God's promises with each lurch and shift.

'Why?' is often our first response when our world is shaken. Why did this happen to me? Why can't I find a job? Why am I ill? Why? But can we really expect our valleys to fill, our mountains and hills to bow low; and our crooked places to be straight and smooth without some shaking?

Instead of asking 'Why?' in life's earthquakes, a better response might be, 'Help me see the salvation of God during the shaking.'

Prayer: *Dear God, help us to see your salvation and feel your presence in each moment of each day. In Jesus' name. Amen*

Thought for the day: How can I reflect the glory of God in unsettling times?

Dana L. Williams (Washington, US)

PRAYER FOCUS: FAMILIES STRUGGLING FINANCIALLY

God's Grace is Sufficient

Read Exodus 18:7–23

[The Lord] said to me, 'My grace is sufficient for you, for my power is made perfect in weakness.'
2 Corinthians 12:9 (NIV)

After a family dinner, I sat at the table with my father-in-law, Darrell, drinking coffee. He rarely talked about his own father; but this afternoon, he told a humorous and touching story about football, a marching band, rain, mud, car heaters and the love of his father. We laughed. I told a similar story about my late father.

The next day, it occurred to me that Darrell has been a father to me for 30 years. When I need help or advice, I turn to him.

Like Jethro, who influenced his son-in-law, Moses, Darrell has influenced me through his caring encouragement and gentle guidance. Darrell is an example of God's grace in my life, and I am learning that God's grace is more than sufficient for me.

God sends people into our lives to bless us and to strengthen us. When we listen for his voice speaking through them, we can grow into the children of God we were meant to be.

Prayer: *Dear God, speak to us through the people we love, as we pray, 'Our Father in heaven, hallowed be your name, your kingdom come, your will be done, on earth as it is in heaven. Give us today our daily bread. And forgive us our debts, as we also have forgiven our debtors. And lead us not into temptation, but deliver us from the evil one.'* Amen*

Thought for the day: Whom is God sending into my life to bless me?

Peter Hyer McNabb (Texas, US)

The Frugal Life

Read Matthew 6:24–34

Look at the birds of the air; they do not sow or reap or store away in barns, and yet your heavenly Father feeds them. Are you not much more valuable than they?
Matthew 6:26 (NIV)

I was standing in a slow-moving supermarket queue, leaning wearily on my shopping trolley as I edged toward the check-out. My eyes fell on the contents of my trolley—piled high with things that weren't really necessary: crisps, sweets, the latest magazine, a pre-prepared meal.

I venture to suggest that many of us can live more frugally. What prompts us to buy so much? Is it simple lack of thought or do we like to hoard? Or perhaps we buy what advertisers tell us we need.

In scripture, Jesus teaches us not to worry about our daily needs, to choose instead to seek God's kingdom above all else. I believe that if our focus were indeed on seeking the righteousness of God, we wouldn't spend so much on ourselves. Perhaps the money we would have spent could be used to help someone in need rather than to fill our own cupboards. And we may well discover that as we give, our own lives are enriched as well.

Prayer: *Help us, O God, to trust in your promise to provide for us as we seek to obey your calling on our lives! Amen*

Thought for the day: How do I honour God in the way I use my resources?

Caryl Moll (Gauteng, South Africa)

Loving the 'Unlovely'

Read Galatians 3:26–29
In Christ Jesus you are all children of God through faith.
Galatians 3:26 (NRSV)

As a school head teacher I used unconsciously to place children into two categories: 'lovely' children (those who were no trouble) and 'unlovely' (difficult) children. One particular first year student was sent to my office nearly every day because his behaviour was so out of control. I began to dislike this child because he spent so much time in my office disrupting my routine. One day his mother failed to pick him up from school, so I drove him home. As we pulled into a run-down caravan park, he pointed to a windowless caravan where rubbish littered the yard and the door was wide open on a freezing cold day. This was his home. His mother appeared at the door and ushered him in. Stunned, I drove away.

How could I discount this child who did not have the comfort of a dry, warm place to live? Didn't he need me more than others? From that day forward, I considered all children to be God's children—not 'lovely' or 'unlovely'. God holds us responsible to take care of each one of his children. When I treat any child carelessly, I am treating Christ carelessly. When I treat each child as a beloved child of God, I am honouring Christ.

Prayer: *Thank you, Father, for your unconditional love. Forgive us when we fail to love your children as you love them. Amen*

Thought for the day: God calls us to love those who are not easy to love.

Matt Stephen (Arkansas, US)

Searching for Jesus

Read Jeremiah 29:11–13
When you search for me… with all you heart, you will find me.
Jeremiah 29:13 (CEB)

My friend Carole has produced an outdoor passion play every summer for 30 years. The entire play hinges on having the right person in the role of Jesus. Many volunteer actors have played that role over the years. Each one in his own way has highlighted attributes that point to the Saviour's gentleness, compassion, love and authority.

With only volunteer actors, some might wonder how Carole consistently locates so many men who can play the key part. But I know that all through the year, everywhere she goes her eyes are open for the person whose actions show he could portray Jesus.

Carole's persistence reminds me of God's words recorded by Jeremiah. Today's verse encourages us to search for God wholeheartedly. We shouldn't restrict our pursuit of him to a few hours on Sunday or a few fleeting minutes in daily prayer but all through our day, everywhere we are. Just as my friend constantly searches for her portrayer of Jesus, we should seek God. And when we search with all of our heart, we will find him.

Prayer: *Dear God, help us to devote ourselves to pursuing you. In the name of Jesus. Amen*

Thought for the day: I will look for God throughout my day today.

Beverly Varnado (Georgia, US)

Gifts from the Heart

Read 2 Corinthians 9:6–14

Since you excel in everything—in faith, in speech, in knowledge, in complete earnestness and in the love we have kindled in you—see that you also excel in this grace of giving.
2 Corinthians 8:7 (NIV)

I have a patch of lavender growing in my back garden. Every time I water it or touch its leaves, I smile and think of the woman who gave it to me nearly ten years ago. She suffered from multiple sclerosis and I was her nurse. I visited her at home a few times, and on my last visit she handed me a bundle of lavender from her garden. When I arrived home I planted it straight away. Ten years later the plant continues to thrive, sprouting beautiful blooms in the spring and summer. This gift lovingly given so many years ago continues to bless my life.

Christians are called to be gracious to one another. This may mean giving material things to those in need or offering support to someone needing encouragement. The best gift we can give is the knowledge and love of Christ. And when we give in Christ's name, God can use what we do today to bless others for years to come.

Prayer: *O God, we thank you for Jesus, your ultimate gift to us. We ask that you help us to be gracious to others in his name. Amen*

Thought for the day: The best gift we'll ever give or receive is the love of Christ.

Michelle S. Lowe (North Carolina, US)

Holy Intermissions

Read Colossians 4:2–6

Devote yourselves to prayer, being watchful and thankful.
Colossians 4:2 (NIV)

When I was growing up in church, we used to sing a hymn about a 'sweet hour of prayer'.* But whenever I tried to pray for an hour I failed—and I felt defeated.

As an adult I no longer try to pray for 60 minutes. What help me are short periods of time with God. Several times a day, I set aside five or ten minutes to focus on my Lord. During one of these brief interludes, I read *The Upper Room*. Another time I'll read a psalm and listen to what the Lord is saying to me. These 'intermissions' become even more meaningful as I look around at God's marvellous creation. I hear the birds and notice the beauty of flowers, and I praise God for his wonderful works. If I am distracted by anxious thoughts, I take a moment to count ten blessings in my life and voice my gratitude to God.

These moments of renewal help me to see each day as God's gift—and my need to honour him on that day. As I continue these spiritual practices, I experience the renewing and nurturing touch of the Spirit of God.

Prayer: *Dear Lord, may we not forget you in our rushed routines. Help us to connect with you throughout each day. Amen*

Thought for the day: Prayer is about a heartfelt desire to draw near to God.

Clifford B. Rawley (Missouri, US)

PRAYER FOCUS: THOSE WHO FEEL TOO BUSY TO PRAY
*William W. Walford, 'Sweet Hour of Prayer,' 1845.

Bouquet

Read Isaiah 40:25–31

Thanks be to God, who in Christ always leads us in triumphal procession, and through us spreads in every place the fragrance that comes from knowing him.

2 Corinthians 2:14 (NRSV)

The day before our Harvest Festival several friends from church and I decorated it with flowers, berries and fruit. Our work went smoothly. Soon, bright arrangements decorated the whole church. When the main decorative work had been completed there were some 'leftovers' on the table—broken branches, squashed flowers and unopened buds. As we gathered all this together to throw it into the bin, the caring hands of one woman took a few items from the pile, wrapped a ribbon around them, and crowned her masterpiece with a shiny bead. A charming bouquet appeared before our eyes.

Sometimes I feel like one of those superfluous, broken branches, thrown overboard in this materially oriented world. But for our Lord none of us is superfluous or unnecessary. Each person is precious and valuable in God's eyes (see Isaiah 43:4). Each of us is a unique flower in the fragrant bouquet of the Lord.

Prayer: *Generous and merciful God, help us to know ourselves as your beloved children. Help us to understand that we are wonderfully made by you and that we have everything we need for life and holiness. Amen*

Thought for the day: None of us is superfluous to God.

Irina Ivanova (Pskov, Russia)

Rest in God's Arms

Read Philippians 4:4–13

The Lord is good, a refuge in times of trouble. He cares for those who trust in him.

Nahum 1:7 (NIV)

Late on the evening of 11 September 2001, I opened my door to two representatives of the New York City Fire Department. They came to tell me that my husband, a fire-fighter, was unaccounted for. With those words, my teenage daughters and I embarked on a journey we had never expected to take.

A few weeks earlier, we had been on holiday at a campsite. A friend's young child had got into trouble, and his dad picked him up to carry him back to the camp. The child wasn't happy and had gone kicking and screaming. God helped me see that whether the child went kicking and screaming or resting in his father's loving arms, he was going on that journey. Now I realised that I had a similar choice: I could rest in the loving arms of my heavenly Father, or I could choose to resist the Lord. Either way, I was on the journey that began with losing my husband.

Through the many years since then, God has carried me. After a time, he put me down to walk. He allowed me to run ahead, and when needed he picked me up again. The Lord has never left me and has proved to be trustworthy over and over again.

Prayer: *All-powerful God, help us to rest in the assurance that your loving arms are strong enough to hold us. Amen*

Thought for the day: In God's arms is the best place to be.

Ann Van Hine (New York, US)

Making a Difference

Read Luke 17:11–19
I press on toward the goal to win the prize for which God has called me heavenward in Christ Jesus.
Philippians 3:14 (NIV)

At breakfast Bill, an old friend of mine, poured out his frustrations. He believed that he wasn't making a difference in his ministry working with men at the prison in his town. The men would make great progress but then abandon it all when they were released. As a result, Bill was discouraged and ready to give up. Then he started talking about a couple of men who had made changes when they got out and were sticking to them. I was able to encourage Bill that he had made a difference for those men, and that was worth it.

It is easy for us to think we haven't made a difference in our ministry. Too often we feel that what we do doesn't matter. But the truth comes from Jesus. He said that whatever we do for anyone in need matters to him. Encouraging someone can significantly change that person's future. And it can significantly change the future of whomever that person influences.

Prayer: *Dear Jesus, remind us today that as we love you more, we can love your people more, too. Amen*

Thought for the day: Anything we do today for others blesses Jesus.

Chad McComas (Oregon, US)

In Sickness or in Health

Read Acts 4:32–35

If one part suffers, every part suffers with it; if one part is honoured, every part rejoices with it.
1 Corinthians 12:26 (NIV)

I never have 'just' a headache, or 'just' a toothache. If any part of my physical body hurts, I know how difficult it is for my other parts to ignore the pain. God designed my body so that if certain parts are injured, other parts will compensate for the injured part. If I strain my knee, soon my hip starts hurting because my hip is using more muscle power to pull the weight that my knee usually carries. On the other hand, if I wake up feeling good, it is because all of my body is doing well, and my whole body can celebrate.

And so it is with the church body—as Paul stated in our Bible verse for today. In close community, when one of us suffers, others also feel the pain and offer comfort. We are not always suffering and can rejoice and celebrate our lives when good things are happening.

No matter what condition we are in, suffering or rejoicing, it is better to go through either state with the help of others. Together, suffering is more bearable, and rejoicing feels even greater. As a member of Christ's Church, I am committed to helping others and rejoicing with others, whether in sickness or in health.

Prayer: *Dear Jesus, thank you for creating your Church as a body that functions together in all things. Help us to be more loving when others suffer and more joyful when they are happy. Amen*

Thought for the day: Jesus calls us to be united, in sickness or in health.

Deanne Ruedemann (Texas, US)

PRAYER FOCUS: SOMEONE WHO IS ILL

Gutters of Grace

Read Isaiah 41:17–20

Let's throw off any extra baggage, get rid of the sin that trips us up, and fix our eyes on Jesus.
Hebrews 12:1–2 (CEB)

In our area fierce summer thunderstorms often drop a large amount of rain in a very short time. The gutters of my house serve a vital function by channelling the rain. However, when my gutters are clogged up with leaves and moss, the rainwater cannot flow freely.

In a way, we are called to be 'gutters', channels of God's love and grace. Yet—like the gutters on the roof of my house—our lives can become filled with debris. When this happens, we fail to be effective channels of God's refreshing and life-giving water. This debris will look slightly different for each of us. Perhaps it is the busyness of our lives or the worries and fears that consume our thinking. Perhaps it is an unwillingness to forgive or unresolved issues from our past. For me, ambition and seeking people's approval often take centre stage in my life.

Anything that causes us to focus on ourselves instead of on God can prevent us from being effective servants. When we regularly ask God to show us this debris and allow him to help us clean it out, we can become channels of his grace.

Prayer: *Dear God, help us to remove from our lives anything that is keeping us from seeing you and the needs of those around us. Amen*

Thought for the day: I want to be a channel of God's love to others.

Joan Campbell (Gauteng, South Africa)

The Blessing of Work

Read Ecclesiastes 5:18–20

Whatever you do, work at it with all your heart, as working for the Lord, not for human masters.
Colossians 3:23 (NIV)

Many of the jobs I did as a youth were arduous and boring; but I was glad to get the work as I needed the money. Now, in my older years, when I join a group on a mission trip, I expect to be on the business end of a shovel, an axe or another tool that requires exertion and my best effort. While my ageing muscles and joints are now taxed to a greater extent, I find satisfaction in the work.

The teacher in Ecclesiastes encourages us to find satisfaction in our labour (Ecclesiastes 5:18). Working for God is the path to fruitful living. Paul also writes: 'We are God's handiwork, created in Christ Jesus to do good works, which God prepared in advance for us to do' (Ephesians 2:10).

In some of my work, I have had trouble finding God's blessing. However, God has patiently waited for me to realise through experience the blessing of doing all work for him. When we work as for the Lord, we find ourselves longing to do more.

Prayer: *Dear Lord, we give thanks for the privilege and blessing of work. Amen*

Thought for the day: Today I will enjoy my work as a gift from God.

Walter N. Maris (Missouri, US)

Becoming One

Read John 17:20–26

Jesus said, 'I no longer call you servants, because a servant does not know his master's business. Instead, I have called you friends.'
John 15:15 (NIV)

After 41 years of marriage, I know what my husband is thinking most of the time and we finish each other's sentences. The Bible says of married people that 'the two will become one flesh. So they are no longer two, but one' (Matthew 19:5–6). That isn't an immediate oneness. Becoming one with a spouse takes shared interests and experiences—time spent talking and doing things together.

Something similar happens with long-time friends. We often know, without being told, what our close friends are thinking and feeling because of shared experiences, interests and conversations. We experience a unity with our closest friends.

Jesus called his disciples friends. Later he prayed for them, 'that they may be one as we are one—I in them and you in me—so that they may be brought to complete unity. Then the world will know that you sent me and have loved them even as you have loved me' (John 17:22–23). Jesus asked God to make us one with him, just as he and the Father are one. But this oneness takes time, conversation and shared experiences with God. We can begin now to talk to Jesus and listen, as good friends do.

Prayer: *Dear Lord Jesus, thank you for the amazing promise that we can be one with you, one with the Father, and one with each other. Amen*

Thought for the day: Unity with God and others is worth working toward and waiting for.

Jane Reid (Oregon, US)

A Damaged Tree

Read Luke 13:6–9

We are hard pressed on every side, but not crushed; perplexed, but not in despair; persecuted, but not abandoned; struck down, but not destroyed.
2 Corinthians 4:8–9 (NIV)

My wife finally planted a papaya tree after wanting one for a very long time. We watched it grow and looked forward to the day we would eat a fruit from it. One afternoon my wife was watering the garden, and the hose lay on the other side of the new papaya tree. She needed more hose, so she yanked. Unfortunately, the hose snapped the trunk clean off. We couldn't reattach the pieces, and the severed top withered. Our hope for a juicy papaya slipped away. But we continue to watch the stump to see whether it will grow a new stem.

Just as the hose unexpectedly damaged the papaya tree, many things can unexpectedly change or damage our lives. Debilitating diseases may scar the body. Broken relationships can lead to broken hearts. Lost jobs and repossessed homes can wipe out years of hard work. Drugs, alcohol and abuse can devastate families for generations.

But God watches over each of us and cares about the brokenness in our lives. The roots of the little papaya tree are still alive in the ground, and the tree may still come back. And with God's help, so can we all.

Prayer: *Dear Lord, help us to always keep our roots deep in you that no matter what happens, we will survive—and not only survive but overcome. Amen*

Thought for the day: When I face hardship or tragedy God can help me overcome it.

Peter Lundell (California, US)

Accepting New Ways

Read Luke 5:36–39
No one pours new wine into old wineskins.
Luke 5:37 (NIV)

After a number of years acting, walking and responding to life in certain ways, I was set in them. So much so that when the Lord asked me to do a new thing, I found it difficult to respond, to act and walk in a different way.

Jesus uses a description of someone who likes old wine and will not try new wine because they are satisfied with the old. But I wasn't satisfied with my old ways. I was running on empty.

In order for the Lord to pour new life into me I had to let go of the old. For the old wineskin was bruised and battered and the new wine the Lord wanted to give me poured away and went to waste. I thought I was beyond repair.

I was so exhausted that one day I found myself drawn by the Holy Spirit to sit by the well of living water with Jesus (see John 4:1–42). I sat there for a whole year, listening, receiving and letting go of my old nature and the person on whom I had come to rely to get me through tough times. Jesus gave me a new wineskin, filled will all the new things he wanted to give me and to do for him. I'm glad that I let go of my old ways!

Prayer: *Dear Lord, thank you that you love us so much that you want to give us new ways of living and serving. Amen*

Thought for the day: I will walk in Jesus' new way today.

Linda Cunningham (Middlesex, England)

Resurrection Faith

Read Romans 8:35–39

Neither death nor life, neither angels nor demons, neither the present nor the future, nor any powers, neither height nor depth, nor anything else in all creation, will be able to separate us from the love of God that is in Christ Jesus our Lord.
Romans 8:38–39 (NIV)

I could hear my son, Raham, sobbing in the next room. We were burying his grandfather Liberto that day. I couldn't think of anything to say to ease his grief, perhaps because I was devastated myself. Dad had been suffering from major depression—hormonal imbalance, the doctor said. I could not accept that Dad had spent the last days of his life battling depression. He had devoted his life to working with indigenous tribes, sharing the gospel in word and deed. I could not help but ask, 'Is this what happens when you have faith?'

Later as I embraced my son, I sensed God saying to me, 'I know it seems that your world has collapsed. But in death, as in life, your dad is mine. I hold him in my hand. I will never let him go, just as I have never let you go.'

At the funeral, I read these words: 'Dying, Christ destroyed our death. Rising, Christ restored our life. Christ will come again in glory. As in baptism Liberto put on Christ, so in Christ may Liberto be clothed with glory.' Joy welled up in my heart through my tears. I knew Dad was alive and well in the bosom of God. My faith had been restored.

Prayer: *God of grace and glory, when we are grieving, help us to remember your promise of eternal life. Amen*

Thought for the day: If I share in Christ's death, I will also share in his resurrection (see Romans 6:5).

Ray Sison (Manila, Philippines)

Pray All Day

Read 1 Thessalonians 5:16–18

Pray without ceasing.
1 Thessalonians 5:17 (NRSV)

I recall the first time I read the verse in 1 Thessalonians that urges us to pray without ceasing. If I pray without ceasing, I thought, how will I have time to accomplish all the other tasks required of me?

After thoughtful consideration, I realised how I could pray throughout the day.

I began to approach my daily tasks with a prayerful heart. I soon found that my work was more enjoyable when I turned it into an opportunity to commune with God. For example, during house cleaning I gave thanks for God's order in my life. As I prepared meals, I prayed for those who would eat at my table and for those who do not have enough to eat. When weeding the garden, I imagined letting go of old hurts and prideful thoughts with each weed I pulled.

Each moment in our lives presents a chance for prayer. I want to take advantage of every opportunity.

Prayer: *Dear Lord, thank you for hearing our prayers. May we always recognise the opportunities that can be turned into moments of communion with you. Amen*

Thought for the day: I will go through my day with a prayerful heart.

Monica A. Andermann (New York, US)

PRAYER FOCUS: THOSE WHO FEEL BURDENED BY RESPONSIBILITY

God Knows Me

Read Psalm 139: 1–4

The Lord said to Jeremiah, 'Before I formed you in the womb, I knew you.'
Jeremiah 1:5 (NIV)

David B. Smith is a common name—so common that once I was not allowed to board a commercial flight because someone with my name was on the US Department of Homeland Security's 'No Fly' list. Fortunately, my date of birth on my driving licence showed that I was decades older than this person, and I was eventually allowed to board the aeroplane.

I used to feel that in a world with billions of people, God didn't know me. I am not famous. Even in my home town, I am not well known. But reading Psalm 139 helped me to realise that God knows who I am. I don't need to show my driving licence to claim my identity with God. Our reading above describes his knowledge of my thoughts, actions and words, while verse 13 of that same psalm depicts his involvement in forming me in my mother's womb. In the text, I learn that God even has a plan for my life (v. 16).

When we are feeling insignificant or unimportant, we can stop and remember the words found in Psalm 139. God considers us important enough to have been involved in our lives even before we were born.

Prayer: *Dear Father, help us to remember that everyone is important to you. Amen*

Thought for the day: God knows and cares for each of us.

David Bonner Smith (Oregon, US)

Don't You Care?

Read Mark 4:35–41

[Jesus] woke up and rebuked the wind, and said to the sea, 'Peace! Be still!' Then the wind ceased, and there was a dead calm.
Mark 4:39 (NRSV)

While driving, I got a flat tyre, and my son and I had to make an emergency stop. Immediately, the car behind me crashed into my car. We waited in shock as the police documented the accident. Two weeks later, someone stole my bag from my office after our church service. Without the documents in that bag, I would no longer be able to serve in the church. I would have to go to my native town to have everything reissued—a process that takes six months. 'Why did these things happen?' I found myself asking God. 'Don't you care about what's happening to me?'

My question echoed the question the disciples asked in today's reading. Since the disciples were professional fishermen we can assume that they did all they could to save the boat. But it was useless. So they called on Christ, who was sleeping next to them.

Two days after my bag was stolen, I received a phone call. 'I've found your documents,' the caller said. 'They were strewn on the ground, and the police had your phone number because of your car accident.' The joy I felt was indescribable. God does care about me. The Lord Jesus is powerful. He is always waiting to help us.

Prayer: *Dear Lord, help us to call on you before, after and during a crisis. Amen*

Thought for the day: The Lord is waiting nearby to answer our pleas.

Pavel Serdukov (Moscow, Russia)

Finding God in Unexpected Places

Read 1 Kings 19:1–13

The Lord your God is in your midst—a warrior bringing victory. He will create calm with his love; he will rejoice over you with singing.
Zephaniah 3:17 (CEB)

After five days spent caring for my father, I was not looking forward to going back to work. I had not slept well, and had nothing to take for lunch. I parked my car in a distant car park and walked to the building. When I arrived, I saw a basket wrapped with a bow sitting on top of the refrigerator; my name was on the attached card, which I opened and read. A colleague wrote that although I was busy taking care of my dad, I should not forget to take care of myself. She had given me a gift basket of luxurious bath products and chocolates.

This reminded me that God appears in our lives in unexpected places. For example, when Elijah was threatened by Queen Jezebel, he fled into the wilderness. He ate a meal prepared by angels, then went into a cave and waited for God to come. God did not appear in the wind, the earthquake or the fire, but in a gentle whisper that reassured Elijah of his worth and his calling. God was there for me today in the words and the gift of a colleague.

Prayer: *Dear God, thank you for loving us and being with us even in places we don't expect to find you. Amen*

Thought for the day: God comes to us in unexpected ways.

Janice Peacemaker (Virginia, US)

A Comforting Companion

Read Hebrews 13:1–6
The Lord himself goes before you and will be with you; he will never leave you nor forsake you. Do not be afraid; do not be discouraged.
Deuteronomy 31:8 (NIV)

My daughter suffered from concussion following an accident and needed me to care for her at home for two months. In the middle of the seemingly endless days and nights of caring for her, God helped me learn about the spiritual gift of being a carer; it is not for the fainthearted; it means being fully present to the one who needs us. A focused heart discerns subtle needs. The care receiver may experience fear, pain, boredom or a combination of all the above. The presence of a loving carer can make long hours easier for the patient to endure.

The road of caring is bone-weary-tiring at times. I know that it was for me. But God sustained me and enabled me to be part of his healing for my daughter. My role gave me a new appreciation for the many carers who are signs of God's promise: '[I] will never leave you nor forsake you.' Whenever we reach out to those who are hurting, we are offering assurance of God's promise.

Prayer: *Loving God, thank you for being our comforting companion. Sustain each of us with the knowledge of your presence. Amen*

Thought for the day: Caring is a gift from God.

Beth A. Palm (Illinois, US)

A Gift from God

Read Matthew 25:34–40

The King will reply [to the righteous], 'Truly I tell you, whatever you did for one of the least of these brothers and sisters of mine, you did for me.'
Matthew 25:40 (NIV)

Recently many Spanish-speaking people have moved into our community. I appreciate the diversity of language and culture and regret that I cannot speak or understand Spanish yet.

One day I was walking to my car after shopping at my local supermarket. Blocking my path was a young woman holding a little girl's hand and carrying a small boy on her hip. She looked me in the eye and began to talk, but I didn't understand a word except 'baby'. I realised that she was probably asking for money to buy food, but I continued to my car, putting my shopping in the boot. I turned around to see that the woman and her children had followed me. I looked at the little boy perched on his mother's hip. Though I could have been frightening to him, he returned my gaze with the most beautiful, loving smile I have ever seen. I felt as though I were gazing into the face of Christ himself.

Then today's quoted verse came to mind, and I knew what I had to do. I gave them a small gift, but I realised after saying, 'Vaya con Dios' ('Go with God') to them—the little Spanish I remembered—that I was the one who had received the greater gift.

Prayer: *Dear God, thank you for the people that you bring into our lives. Help us to see others through your love and know they are your children and our brothers and sisters. In Jesus' name. Amen*

Thought for the day: It is a blessing to love those whom God brings into my path.

Robert McClure Terhune (Tennessee, US)

Remembering God

Read Psalm 78:1–8

We will tell to the coming generation the glorious deeds of the Lord, and his might, and the wonders that he has done.
Psalm 78:4 (NRSV)

I found studying Greek very difficult. When I finally asked for help, the professor suggested that when I felt overwhelmed, I could look back at what I had already learned. In hindsight, everything I had been taught or worked out for myself seemed easy. Comforted by what I had already accomplished, I was able to press on with my studies.

Psalm 78 gives a brief history of Israel, showing where God had been faithful in Israel's past. The psalmist remembers the history of Israel to tell future generations how God has helped them in the past and to encourage them to continue to trust him. Similar to my teacher's suggestion, the psalmist's description of Israel's perseverance was meant to help the people press on in faith, placing their trust in God.

In life we are often preoccupied with our current situation, asking God to help us at that moment. However, this psalm is a perfect example of why we need to be thankful and remember what God has done for us. As the psalm shows, God's strength is not fleeting. We can remember what he has already helped us to overcome, and it will strengthen us for the future.

Prayer: *Dear God, help us to remember everything that you have done for us and be our comfort in future times. Amen*

Thought for the day: God's faithfulness endures for ever.

Taylor Murray (Ontario, Canada)

Prepare the Way!

Read Matthew 3:1–6
Prepare the way for the Lord, make straight paths for him.
Matthew 3:3 (NIV)

Spiders like to build webs outside our front door. They string their sticky strands from the roof on one side to the large rhododendron on the other, so there's no way around them. Since I'm often the first to leave our house, I'm usually the one to clear away the spiders' webs. This prepares the way for my wife, who comes out after me.

This simple act reminds me of John the Baptist, who came before Jesus and prepared the way for him. But John's preparing the way was spiritual rather than physical. He was commissioned to announce Jesus' coming.

I'm no John the Baptist, so I won't go around preaching 'prepare the way for the Lord'. But I still want my life to honour Jesus and draw others to him. Whether we're with family, neighbours or work colleagues, we can reflect the image of Christ by our actions. Our love, kindness and integrity may give us a chance to share the reason for our hope (see 1 Peter 3:15). We may even reflect our faith with strangers we meet as we shop or travel. For example, when we hold open a door for someone and that person thanks us, we can smile and say, 'You're welcome. God bless you.'

Jesus has already come to this earth, but he promised to come again (see John 14:3). By reflecting him in everything we do, we can prepare the way for his second coming.

Prayer: *Dear heavenly Father, help us to live so others are drawn to Jesus, and give us words to share our hope in you. Amen*

Thought for the day: Our godly lives and actions can draw others to Jesus.

Milton G. Harris (Washington, US)

Faith and Worldliness

Read Philippians 3:18–21
*I thank my God through Jesus Christ for all of you, because your faith is
being reported all over the world.*
Romans 1:8 (NIV)

In the first century, Rome was the most influential city in the world.
While earthly wealth, wisdom and abundant pleasures cause many
believers to grow lukewarm or to fall away from their faith, the
Roman believers remained strong. Their faith was so strong that
the world at large took notice. Paul wrote to them: 'I thank my
God through Jesus Christ for all of you, because your faith is being
reported all over the world' (Romans 1:8). What a testimony for
future generations!

What would Paul say to me? Would he commend me or would
he see that I have put too much confidence in my worldly possessions? In our reading for today, Paul cautions us to focus on Christ's
desires for our lives and not on all the earthly pleasures that sur-
round us. The treasure that is our faith in Christ should far outshine
all the world has to offer.

Prayer: *Dear Lord, give us faith strong enough to shine a spotlight on
you in the midst of all the shiny treasures in the world. Amen*

Thought for the day: Christ's example keeps us focused on living
faithfully.

Kimberly Harms (Iowa, US)

The Word of God

Read 2 Timothy 3:14–17
All Scripture is God-breathed and is useful for teaching, rebuking, correcting and training in righteousness.
2 Timothy 3:16 (NIV)

Life had become so busy that I began just to read the writers' meditations and leave out the Bible passage in my time spent daily reading *The Upper Room.* As helpful and pertinent as all the meditations are, however, they are no substitute for reading the word of God. Missing out the Bible passage is like trying to learn a foreign language from a phrase book. You could get by in a foreign country for a while with set phrases and questions, but you would lack the depth of understanding, knowledge of vocabulary and grammar to communicate meaningfully for very long or to develop proper relationships. I soon felt that I was thirsting for God's word and returned to reading the Bible passages more carefully, meditating on what God had to say to me. Only together with God's word can the writers' thoughts bring us in touch with our loving God.

I have realised that the busier we are the more important it is to put aside time to be with God in Bible study and prayer, to find the strength, protection, guidance and peace we need to deal with all that life throws at us.

Prayer: *Dear heavenly Father, encourage us to read and study your word and to share what we have learned with others. Amen*

Thought for the day: Today I will make time to study my Bible and pay attention to God through his word.

Faith Ford (Herefordshire, England)

Transformations

Read Romans 12:1–3
[God] who began a good work in you will carry it on to completion until the day of Christ Jesus.
Philippians 1:6 (NIV)

After several months of planning to remodel our kitchen, my wife and I began all the removing, tearing out, plastering, hanging, painting and installing. In the end, we were pleased with the results.

When it was finished, I reflected on the passage quoted above. I realised that the weeks of work we devoted to transforming our kitchen was nothing compared to the time and effort God puts into transforming my life. I am a work in progress, being transformed over a lifetime—day by day—by a loving God.

We seek God's transformation when we read and meditate on the scriptures, taking the time to discern what thoughts, attitudes and actions do not bring glory to God and then praying about them. When I am impatient with others, remembering God's kindness brings me a peace that helps me respond in love instead of anger. When I pray for those who frustrate me, God's Spirit replaces my contempt with compassion. The job of transforming each of us is not over, but I am assured that God will complete the work begun in us—replacing our old ways with 'what is good and acceptable and perfect' (Romans 12:2, NRSV).

Prayer: *Dear God, help us to accept the challenges in our lives as you transform us to make us more like you. Amen*

Thought for the day: I can't wait to see how God will work in my life today!

John Bagdanov (California, US)

The Gift of Emotion

Read Luke 19:41–46

As [Jesus] approached Jerusalem and saw the city, he wept over it.
Luke 19:41 (NIV)

Growing up I often experienced negative consequences when I expressed my feelings. So I dampened my exuberance and stifled my anger and sadness, hoping to make life easier. Unfortunately, numbing my emotions through overeating eventually led to obesity and the host of social and health challenges that accompany that condition.

Then I began to notice how Jesus displayed his feelings in scripture. He experienced the full range of human emotion: anger with the moneychangers in the Temple (see John 2:15), grief over the death of his friend Lazarus (see John 11:35) and joy in teaching his disciples (see John 15:11). Jesus allowed himself to be fully, deeply human whether in joy or suffering. This observation gave me the courage to begin to 'feel my feelings' while in the safety of Jesus' company in prayer. Gradually, I was able to experience my feelings as they occurred and to understand them as good gifts from God.

Expressing our emotions is part of the abundance of life to which Jesus invites us. When we express ourselves authentically, it is a gift to God, to ourselves and to the world.

Prayer: *Dear God, help us to continue to learn and grow so that we may be more effective in our ministries. Amen*

Thought for the day: What emotional risk can God empower me to take today?

Margaret Gillikin (Colorado, US)

The Man in the Shop

Read Matthew 22:34–40

Whatever good we do, we will receive the same again from the Lord.
Ephesians 6:8 (NRSV)

When I was roaming around the music section in a shop one day, an older man on a mobility scooter almost ran into me. 'Sorry about that,' he said to me, 'How are you today?' I was surprised for a second, but I responded and we went on to have a long conversation in one of the aisles at the shop.

The rest of the day I thought about the friendly man. I wondered whether I had made a difference to his day. Then it dawned on me that he had made a big difference to my day. The idea that someone would stop in the middle of the hustle and bustle of a large shop and talk to a young teenager made me think. God can use anyone to touch others' lives, regardless of age, personality, intelligence, faith tradition or any other trait. Whatever the circumstances, we can always raise someone's spirits. Even just smiling or listening can make someone's day. I have resolved to watch for these opportunities that God has set out for me.

Prayer: *Dear Lord, we pray for you to help us be nice to everyone we meet and to pray for them. Amen*

Thought for the day: How is God calling me to make a difference in someone's life today?

James Hubbard (Texas, US)

PRAYER FOCUS: A FRIEND OF A DIFFERENT GENERATION

Let Them Go

Read 1 Peter 1:3–9

Cast all your anxiety on [God] because he cares for you.
1 Peter 5:7 (NIV)

While on an early morning walk, I felt a gentle breeze. Ahead I noticed hundreds of leaves falling from the nearby trees. At first my heart sank when I thought about the return of winter with its ice and cold temperatures. But as I watched the reds, oranges and yellows circle in the air and drift down, I sensed a gentle reminder. 'Let the burdens go. Make room for what I have planned for you.'

The trees drop their leaves in autumn, making room for the new spring buds. In the same way, I can let go of my burdens, troubles and cares to make room for the fresh blessings God has in store for me. I can place those cares into his hands. When I thought of these assurances that day, my steps became lighter and my heart was filled with peace. We can have that same peace—from the same source—every day.

Prayer: *Dear Father, help us to give you all of our cares and troubles to make room for the new life that you offer. We pray as Jesus taught us, saying, 'Our Father which art in heaven, Hallowed be thy name. Thy kingdom come. Thy will be done, as in heaven, so in earth. Give us day by day our daily bread. And forgive us our sins; for we also forgive every one that is indebted to us. And lead us not into temptation; but deliver us from evil.'* Amen*

Thought for the day: Every care that I can turn over to God makes room for another blessing.

Sharon Beth Brani (Virginia, US)

All One in Christ Jesus

Read Mark 9: 38–40

[Jesus prayed]: 'I pray also for those who will believe in me through their message, that all of them may be one, Father, just as you are in me and I am in you.'
John17:20–21 (NIV)

I had the privilege of attending two remarkable commemorations some time ago. On 3 August 1913 fire broke out in Cadder No. 15 pit, then part of the Lanarkshire coalfields in Scotland. Twenty-two men lost their lives that day; eleven were Roman Catholic and eleven Protestant. A monument bearing the names of the Catholics was erected two miles west of the pit, and another to the Protestants was erected two miles in the opposite direction. Sadly, neither memorial mentioned the other eleven men.

One hundred years to the day all that changed when a memorial to all 22 miners was unveiled at a local cemetery. The service was led by a Baptist minister and the singing by a Salvation Army band. The following day a second memorial was unveiled outside the local library; this time the service was conducted by a Church of Scotland minister and a Roman Catholic priest. On each occasion large crowds gathered to pay their respects, some of them descendants of the men killed so long ago.

How good it is when Christians of all denominations can join together, regardless of the differences in their observance. How much better it will be when, as Jesus prayed, 'all of them may be one'.

Prayer: *Dear Lord, we thank you for the Bible and its teachings on fellowship and love. Help us to put it into practice in our own Christian communities. Amen*

Thought for the day: How can we show our love for those of other denominations?

William Findlay (Lanarkshire, Scotland)

Plan B

Read Romans 15:20–28

Since I have been longing for many years to visit you, I plan to do so when I go to Spain… and to have you assist me on my journey there… Now, however, I am on my way to Jerusalem in the service of the Lord's people there.

Romans 15:23–25 (NIV)

Often my Plan A falls through and I have to go with Plan B. Before graduation, my 'humble' Plan A was first to pastor a 2000-member church and then work my way up from there. I landed in Plan B: a country church with 38 members. It was the best thing that could have happened, giving my wife and me the chance to focus on establishing our marriage. When I retired, my Plan A was to hike through the forests of southern Oregon. Then I started experiencing foot problems. Plan B became rewarding pastoral work and representing abused children in court.

Paul's Plan A was to plant churches in Spain. He landed in prison. His Plan B: he wrote Ephesians, Philippians, Colossians and Philemon, by which millions have been blessed. Ruth's Plan A was to live quietly in Moab with her foreign husband. When her husband died, a new plan emerged and she moved to Israel, becoming an ancestor of Jesus. Her faith and commitment became an inspiration to millions.

We all make plans and suffer disappointment when those plans don't come to fruition. I've learned that however grand our goals, God might have deeper spiritual opportunities in store for us that can turn our disappointment into joy.

Prayer: *Guardian of our lives, in the midst of frustration, help us to believe that you have greater plans for us than we even know to dream.*

Thought for the day: Today, I will look for the Plan B opportunities that God brings my way.

George Nye (Oregon, US)

Childhood Memories

Read Isaiah 66:7–13

The Lord says, 'As a mother comforts her child, so I will comfort you.'
Isaiah 66:13 (NRSV)

Our daughter was six years old when we told her that the parents of her best friend were divorcing. Soon she began to cry. We tried to console her. I had no idea what to do. Eventually, I gathered her in my arms and walked outside into the warm night. I don't remember what I said, if anything. In time, she rested her head on my shoulder, and we simply gazed at the bright moon.

I had forgotten that painful yet tender moment. But over 30 years later, my daughter became the foster parent of a child who would cry at night because he missed his mother. My daughter told me she tried to console the little boy but to no avail. Remembering her own childhood heartache, she held him and took him outside. Together, they looked at the moon as she tried to comfort the child. In time, the child's sobbing subsided.

I think of those times in our lives when God touches us with love and grace in moments of hurt and uncertainty. Those memories bring comfort and peace as well as thanksgiving and humility that God would intervene in the life of a parent trying to comfort their child.

Prayer: *Loving Father, thank you for being present in our lives always. Amen*

Thought for the day: When life seems hopeless, God's steadfastness gives us hope.

Gary Story (Kentucky, US)

PRAYER FOCUS: CHILDREN IN FOSTER CARE

Comfort Comes from Christ

Read 2 Corinthians 1:1–7

[God] consoles us in all our affliction, so that we may be able to console those who are in any affliction with the consolation with which we ourselves are consoled by God.

2 Corinthians 1:4 (NRSV)

I had suffered from deep depression since my early teens and had attempted suicide several times. Eventually I was sent to hospital for drug addiction and was not allowed to leave the hospital for at least three months. In despair, I prayed, 'Lord, nothing will come of my own strength. I am afraid of the people here. Please save me.'

The answer to my prayers came from scripture. When I read 2 Corinthians 1:1–7, the suffering of Jesus was revealed to me. In my own suffering, I had forgotten it. Recognising that I had been focusing only on my own troubles, I prayed, 'Jesus, I am sorry. Please help me to feel your presence again.' I was given peace and reassured that God is with us even in the midst of our pain.

I received a charge that no matter what my circumstances, I should think about the suffering of Christ. So I pray that in the future, when I meet people in circumstances similar to my own, I will not hesitate to support them.

Prayer: *Dear Lord, we give you thanks for the comfort we receive from you. Lead us to people whom we can console. Amen*

Thought for the day: Because Christ suffered, he can comfort me when I suffer.

Kaeko Satoru (Chiba, Japan)

Hear the Message

Read Psalm 85:8–13
Faith comes from hearing the message, and the message is heard through the word about Christ.
Romans 10:17 (NIV)

In my devotional time, my habit has always been to read the Bible passage quietly to myself. But recently I found myself needing to reread each passage several times. I began to realise that I was just allowing my eyes to scan across the page. I was not really paying attention to what I read and I definitely was not hearing its message. So I began to read the scripture verses out loud. But as I did, I noticed that I would inadvertently change a word, skip a word or even insert a word. I realised that I must have skipped even more words when reading silently. No wonder I'd had trouble understanding the message before!

Reading aloud also gives me the opportunity to add expression to the scripture verses. It allows me to hear and feel the emotions of the passage. It has become easier to understand the message because I am able to hear God's word to me.

We may have the opportunity to hear God's word many times during the week: during worship services and Bible studies, in the songs we sing or when we read our daily Bible passages. When we hear and begin to understand God's message, our faith surely grows stronger.

Prayer: *Dear God, open our eyes to read your word. Open our ears to hear your voice. Open our hearts to accept your love. Amen*

Thought for the day: How can I hear God's message anew today?

Janet Pierce (Tennessee, US)

PRAYER FOCUS: PEOPLE LEARNING TO READ

Why Didn't You Answer?

Read Mark 1:16–20

Jonah ran away from the Lord.
Jonah 1:3 (NIV)

Sometimes when our son was playing outside he would act as though he hadn't heard when his mother called him. Once she asked him, 'Why didn't you answer me?' With remarkable honesty he replied, 'I thought if I pretended I couldn't hear you, then you might leave me alone.'

Many times we treat God in the same way. He has called us, yet often we pretend not to hear. We ignore the Spirit who is nudging us in a certain direction through scripture, or we turn away when we sense the urge to speak to someone or offer a helping hand to a stranger. We are God's creation, yet he has given us the freedom to choose to turn away from opportunities to serve.

For years, out of fear or busyness, I made the choice to turn away. But turning away left a separation between God and me. Something was missing, and life felt incomplete. I finally realised that I could draw close to God by responding to the nudges and calls. The first few times were scary. But I followed God's leading and now give thanks for the blessings this has brought me. My relationship with God brings a whole new dimension of fullness to life. Hobbies, leisure activities and even work tasks take on new meaning and joy when we do them to praise God.

Prayer: *Dear Lord, open our ears to hear your call and direct our feet in paths of service to you. Amen*

Thought for the day: Choosing to serve God brings light and joy into each day.

Gale A. Richards (Iowa, US)

Deep-Rooted Faith

Read Ephesians 3:13–21

Continue to live your lives in [Christ Jesus], rooted and built up in him and established in the faith, just as you were taught, abounding in thanksgiving.

Colossians 2:6–7 (NRSV)

Here in Texas, it can get very dry and stay that way for a long time. Many plants that grow well in the wet spring wither and die because they aren't drought resistant. But there are always some plants that continue to grow no matter how long drought lasts, because their roots grow deep and reach down to sources of water underground. This allows them to outlast the worst droughts.

In life, we often face a similar situation. When life is good, we can sometimes forget how much God does for us. It is only when we have problems—the 'droughts' of life—that our faith is truly tested. If our faith in God is shallow, when the going gets tough, our faith does not grow. But if we have a deeply rooted relationship with God, then we can outlast any problem this world can bring. With this kind of faith we know that God is with us even when we are facing the worst circumstances. No matter what, God's living water runs deep and never fails.

Prayer: *All-powerful God, when life has made us weak, help us to have the faith to depend upon your strength. Amen*

Thought for the day: With God, sometimes the lowest point in life can be the strongest point in life.

Mark A. Carter (Texas, US)

Using One's Wealth

Read Matthew 27:57–60

As for those who in the present age are rich, command them not to be haughty, or to set their hopes on the uncertainty of riches, but rather on God who richly provides us with everything for our enjoyment.
1 Timothy 6:17 (NRSV)

Joseph of Arimathea was a wealthy man who had become a disciple of Jesus. He did not allow his money to become his idol, his reason for living or a replacement for Jesus. He used his wealth for the purpose of serving Christ, even at a time of deep grief for Jesus' followers. Joseph took the body of Christ, wrapped it in clean linen and placed it in a new tomb that Joseph had made for himself. Having one's own tomb was reserved for the wealthy, not for a common man killed on a cross.

How much money we have doesn't matter. What matters is how we use what we have. What a good example Joseph is for us today, both for those who have a great deal of money and for those whose pockets are empty! Loving Jesus gives us a purpose and an inheritance far greater than any bank account. May our love for Christ prompt us to live generously for his sake.

Prayer: *Generous God, let our desire be only to serve you. Inspire us to use our resources for your glory by helping those in need. Amen*

Thought for the day: It's not about how much we have but how we use what we have to serve God.

Malinda Fillingim (North Carolina, US)

Which Way, Lord?

Read Psalm 119:1–8

Trust in the Lord with all your heart and lean not on your own understanding; in all your ways submit to him, and he will make your paths straight.

Proverbs 3:5–6 (NIV)

I drive customers home or to work when they leave their cars for service or repair at our garage. I never know whether I might be driving to family neighbourhoods, commercial districts or industrial estates. Some areas have straight roads and some are winding. All have side streets leading from the main path.

This situation reminds me of the spiritual roads we travel. Sometimes as we cruise through life, making our daily decisions is easy and unambiguous. At other times life is full of twists and turns and the road ahead looks ominous. Many times we take the side street that appears to be promising only to discover that looks can, indeed, be deceiving—and we end up where we have no business being. At other times we avoid the path that we may perceive as menacing or difficult to manoeuvre and miss the rewards that were waiting for us there.

God wants to direct our course in life as we strive to follow the true path of righteousness. To that end, he gives us discernment through our prayers and reading the Bible. When we know the Lord, making those difficult decisions becomes easier.

Prayer: *Dear God, may we always seek your will and direction for our lives and may we have the faith to follow. Amen*

Thought for the day: The better we know God, the better we can choose the right path.

Thomas Jones (Florida, US)

PRAYER FOCUS: DRIVERS ON UNFAMILIAR ROADS

God is with Us

Read Isaiah 43:1–7

When you pass through the waters, I will be with you; and through the rivers, they shall not overwhelm you; when you walk through fire you shall not be burned, and the flame shall not consume you. For I am the Lord your God, the Holy One of Israel, your Saviour.
Isaiah 43:2–3 (NRSV)

Australia is a land of sweeping plains, rugged mountain ranges, droughts and flooding rains. Our region had experienced years of drought. Then last summer three floods came across our farm in a three-month period. We were safe but surrounded by water. We did not lose any livestock, but we did lose crops, which left us with a financial loss. Fences and roads were swept away and debris was left everywhere. The clean-up kept us busy for months.

My eyes were opened when I read today's reading from Isaiah: 'When you pass through the waters, I will be with you' (v. 2)—'when' not 'if'! We will pass through waters and walk through fire; but God promises, 'I am the Lord your God… your Saviour… Do not fear, for I am with you' (vv. 3, 5). We can trust in God because he is faithful. When we realise what God has done for us, we don't need to be afraid of whatever disasters happen in the world. God has formed us and called us by name. He loves us, redeems us and blots out our sins. What a privilege to belong to such a great and gracious God!

Prayer: *We love you, Lord. When the flood and fire comes, we are thankful for your presence with us. What a comfort it is to know that you are our God, the Holy One, our Saviour! Amen*

Thought for the day: God is always with us.

Janine Randell (New South Wales, Australia)

A Prayer of Repentance

Read Psalm 103:1–12

If we confess our sins, he is faithful and just to forgive us our sins, and to cleanse us from all unrighteousness.
1 John 1:9 (KJV)

I was a chaplain to the inmates at the prison near my home. One day, a prisoner told me that he had difficulty in forgiving himself for past sins. I inquired if he had asked for God's forgiveness and if he believed that God had forgiven him. He said that he had.

'Then you must forgive yourself,' I concluded.

Memories—both good and bad—are stored in our brain and resurface from time to time. We find pleasure in reminiscing about good events, but we are uncomfortable when we recall bad ones. However, they lose their power when we remember the words of the psalmist, 'as far as the east is from the west, so far hath [the Lord] removed our transgressions from us' (Psalm 103:12). When memories bring us guilt, we can remember God's forgiveness and unconditional love. His love is our refuge at all times, and he has promised us peace.

Prayer: *Thank you, God, for Jesus Christ, who died for our sins. Forgive us our sins, and cleanse us from all unrighteousness. Amen*

Thought for the day: God wants us to have peace in our hearts.

Lyle F. Weldon (Kentucky, US)

Well Done

Read Matthew 20:1–16
The last will be first, and the first will be last.
Matthew 20:16 (NIV)

My father was diagnosed with terminal cancer shortly before I left home to go to college. When the time came for me to leave I felt scared and burdened. I prayed many prayers for him to accept Christ as his Saviour and to be healed. Two years later, my father lost his battle with kidney cancer.

After my father's death, I learned that an elderly preacher who lived in a town near where my father was frequently in hospital had been visiting him. My father found him to be a likeable, caring friend—gentle and soft-spoken. When my father was released to come home from the hospital, the preacher travelled almost an hour each way to visit him on Sunday afternoons. On several occasions the preacher talked with my father about Christ and heaven. Shortly before my father passed away, he accepted Christ as his Saviour.

Recently, while reading Matthew 20, I recognised my father's story in it. The meaning of this parable was suddenly deeper and more profound. My father was like the last workers hired. His acceptance of Christ came late in his life, but I know that he was joyfully received by the Saviour.

Prayer: *Dear God, help us to understand your word, to apply it to our lives and to keep it in our hearts. Amen*

Thought for the day: No matter when we turn to Christ, he joyfully receives us.

Sherry Stout-Stewart (North Carolina, US)

Never Old or Damaged

Read 2 Corinthians 4:7–18

We do not lose heart. Even though our outer nature is wasting away, our inner nature is being renewed day by day.
2 Corinthians 4:16 (NRSV)

I recall a lovely flowering tree standing beside a bridge near the main road in my town. What a sight to behold! One morning workmen cut down the tree in order to widen the road. Only the stump remained. How sad! The beautiful flowering tree was gone.

More than 40 years have passed, and the tree has refused to die. The stump grew into a tree even more beautiful than before. Its branches are strong, and now we gaze again upon the beautiful tree with red flowers.

We too experience tribulations and illnesses. Our outer nature may change because of damaging life experiences. But through our faith in God, we are renewed day by day.

Prayer: *Thank you, Father, for being our constant companion in whatever challenges life brings us as we pray, 'Our Father which art in heaven, Hallowed be thy name. Thy kingdom come. Thy will be done in earth, as it is in heaven. Give us this day our daily bread. And forgive us our debts, as we forgive our debtors. And lead us not into temptation, but deliver us from evil: For thine is the kingdom, and the power and the glory, for ever.'* Amen*

Thought for the day: When life cuts us down, God restores and renews us.

Myriam Figueroa Ramírez (Luquillo, Puerto Rico)

Lay Down your Burden

Read Job 38:1–12

[Jesus said] 'Come to me, all you who are weary and burdened, and I will give you rest.'
Matthew 11:28 (NIV)

It's hard to imagine anyone having such a traumatic time as Job does. He worshipped God, was faithful to him and was a good man, shunning evil. He was extremely wealthy, with a large family and many animals. He lost everything and his own health suffered. But despite everything that happened to him, Job still praised God: 'The Lord gave and the Lord has taken away; may the name of the Lord be praised' (Job 1:21).

It was in these hard times for Job that God spoke to him in chapters 38—40. In wonderful descriptions of creation, God reminds Job of all he has created, from light and darkness to donkeys and ostriches. Job realises that God is God, in control of his creation. At the end of the book we read that God blessed the last part of Job's life even more than the first part. His burdens were gone.

Sometimes we, like Job, feel overwhelmed by what happens to us. Our shoulders droop, our feet feel leaden and we fear we might collapse under the weight of the burden we carry. Then we too can remember not only God's control of his world, but that Jesus has invited us to leave our burdens at his feet and rest in his presence.

Prayer: *Lord Jesus, you understand the burdens that we carry. Help us to lay them at your feet and to rest in your presence. Amen*

Thought for the day: To leave my burdens with Jesus today.

Pam Pointer (Wiltshire, England)

An Offer You Can't Refuse

Read John 4:28–42

[The healed blind man] answered them, 'I have told you already, and you would not listen. Why do you want to hear it again? Do you also want to become his disciples?'

John 9:27 (NRSV)

I am a gadget man. When I discover a new electronic device or software, I get excited. Recently I found a free scheduling app for my tablet that would send reminders about project-due dates and help me to plan my work and hold myself accountable. I told my wife, Bonnie, about it and downloaded it to her tablet. Then I sent emails to my three children, urging them to download it quickly, since it would go back to full price the next day.

This zeal to share good news is a smaller version of the fervour that wells up in us when we receive Christ. What a treasure we've found! We feel buoyant, free from guilt. Immediately we wonder if others are like us, feeling the pain of guilt. I have discovered just what they need, something they literally can't live without. Christ offers freedom from guilt, the power to overcome and daily fellowship with God. What's more we now have a new understanding of scripture and ultimately a home in heaven. This is priceless! I want to share this good news.

Prayer: *Dear Lord, give us a renewed desire to share the good news. Amen*

Thought for the day: 'Go into all the world and proclaim the good news to the whole creation' (Mark 16:15).

Tom Buice (Tennessee, US)

When We Have No Words

Read Romans 8:18–27

The Spirit helps us in our weakness. We do not know what we ought to pray for, but the Spirit himself intercedes for us through wordless groans.
Romans 8:26 (NIV)

Ordinarily, my wife gets out of bed to attend to our four young children. Recently, I happened to get out of bed before my wife. After helping the older children, I made every attempt to get our 18-month-old son what he wanted for breakfast. He pointed at the cupboard and pronounced, 'Muhh!' I had no idea what he was asking for. I opened the refrigerator. He pointed and cried, 'Chehhh!' I offered him pudding, egg and waffles, but he only became more frustrated. Finally, I woke his mother and explained the situation. She promptly replied, 'He wants milk and a slice of cheese.' She understands him even when he doesn't have the words.

I couldn't understand my son, but God understands even the groanings of our hearts. He knows our needs, hurts and longings. Even when we have no words to speak, we can turn to God and know that he will understand.

Prayer: *Amazing God, let our hearts never grow silent, even when we have no words to say. Amen*

Thought for the day: God understands our prayers even when we don't have the words.

Chris Surber (Florida, US)

God is with Us Today

Read Psalm 139:5–18

You hem me in, behind and before, and lay your hand upon me. Such knowledge is too wonderful for me; it is so high that I cannot attain it.
Psalm 139:5–6 (NRSV)

The daily devotion in *The Upper Room* that day was about a woman who, like me, loves maps. I have a map of the world on my wall, and I keep an atlas and a street directory on my bookshelf. I don't travel a lot; but I love to know where the people I read about are living.

My maps help me feel connected to others, but God doesn't need a map to know us. Psalm 139 assures us that he is familiar with all our ways—that before a word leaves our tongue he knows it completely (v. 4). What a comfort in times of distress is the reminder in verse 12: 'Even the darkness is not dark to you; the night is as bright as the day, for darkness is as light to you'!

Our granddaughter is about to travel on her own to the other side of the world. I am fearful for her safety, but I am confident that God will accompany her wherever she goes. I hold on to verses 9–10: 'If I take the wings of the morning and settle at the farthest limits of the sea, even there your hand shall lead me, and your right hand shall hold me fast.'

Prayer: *Dear God, when we are disoriented, remind us that you can lead us home because you know us well. We are grateful for your unfailing love. Amen*

Thought for the day: In our times of darkness, we can remember that for God, 'the night is as bright as the day' (Psalm 139:12).

Beverly Dykes (New South Wales, Australia)

Be Bold!

Read 1 Peter 3:13–17

Let your light shine before others, that they may see your good deeds and glorify your Father in heaven.
Matthew 5:16 (NIV)

Autumn is a wonderful season in Tennessee. On many days the temperature is just right. My lunch hour gives me a great opportunity to go outdoors and enjoy a break from the office.

Sometimes I settle at a table outside a café or retreat to a shady spot near bubbling fountains to enjoy my time alone. I often carry with me a small Bible and take in not only physical nourishment but food for my spirit as well.

After a particularly challenging morning at work, I settled wearily in a sunny spot, being careful to hide my Bible. I didn't want passersby to think I was a religious fanatic. I began to feel my spirits lift as I let God's peace and presence wash away my stress. Then I noticed a young man across the way reading a big, thick book—the Bible. A few minutes later, a young woman sat down at another table and opened her Bible. They made no effort to hide what they were reading, as I had done. What a wonderful example they were for me to follow—to show others my commitment to growing in my faith.

Prayer: *Dear God, give us the strength and the power through your Holy Spirit to be bold in our faith as we walk this journey. Amen*

Thought for the day: Today I will look for ways to show my faith to others.

Wilma Vernich (Tennessee, US)

Grandmother's Favourite

Read Matthew 5:43–48

[Your Father] makes the sun rise on both the evil and the good and sends rain on both the righteous and the unrighteous… Therefore, just as your heavenly Father is complete in showing love to everyone, so also you must be complete.
Matthew 5:45, 48 (CEB)

My sister has three grandsons, all nearly grown up now. When the boys were young and for years afterwards, she told each one that he was her favourite. Because she always did this within earshot of the others, the three boys grew up knowing that their grandmother loved them equally.

God loves us similarly. But we sometimes fall into believing that only we are blessed, and we too readily look down on other people. Or, we wonder why others' prayers are being answered immediately when ours are delayed. And when we do so, we miss the mark, forgetting God's abundant and equal love.

For me, it is as simple as recalling the song, 'Jesus loves me! This I know, for the Bible tells me so.' Yes, God loves me. And at the same time, he loves everyone else. We can do well when we accept God's love as my sister's grandsons accepted her love, knowing that all of us are loved equally.

Prayer: *Dear Lord, help us to accept your love gratefully and enable us to love others as you love them. Amen*

Thought for the day: God loves us all equally.

Steve Collier (Kentucky, US)

PRAYER FOCUS: TO ACCEPT GOD'S LOVE

A Forgotten Prayer Request

Read James 5:13–16
Is anyone among you in trouble? Let them pray.
James 5:13 (NIV)

'Please pray for me and my family,' said Laxmi, her eyes filled with tears. 'I belong to a non-Christian family and praying to your God is forbidden in my house. My husband is critically ill.' I assured her that I would indeed pray for her family. She mentioned the names of other family members and her belief that Christ can do miracles. But I forgot to pray for Laxmi. As a busy doctor, I loaded my prayers with petitions for my own family and my patients, and Laxmi was just a face in the crowd, easily forgotten.

A couple of months later, Laxmi came to thank me for praying for her family and said that her husband was on the road to recovery. I was embarrassed to receive her thanks when I had actually forgotten to pray for her. At that moment I asked Laxmi to sit with me and we prayed together for her husband and her family.

We often tend to forget our neighbours and those in trouble—even those who seek us out and request our prayers. It takes effort to live as a Christian, especially in India where we are only about two per cent of the population. But it's worth it because we can make a difference in the lives of those around us as we pray for those in need.

Prayer: *Dear Lord Jesus, we thank you for teaching us to pray. Help us to use prayer to bring more people to you. Amen*

Thought for the day: When someone asks me for prayer, I will not forget.

Leena Vijaykumar (Karnataka, India)

Thirsty Hands

Read John 4:7–14

I spread out my hands to you; I thirst for you like a parched land.
Psalm 143:6 (NIV)

As autumn gave way to winter, I had noticed that my hands were feeling tighter. My cuticles were cracking, and the areas between my fingers were dry. Throughout the day I found myself frequently applying moisturiser. One morning it finally dawned on me: this was not an external problem but an internal one. My skin was dry because I was not drinking enough water.

During different seasons, our internal spiritual lives can also show external signs of thirst. When the cares of life increase, our reading and studying of God's word may decrease. A once-fervent prayer life can experience drought. The joy of our salvation can be diminished by stress and frustration. In times like these, our spirit cries out in thirst 'like a parched land'.

As Jesus promised in today's reading, spiritual thirst is quenched when we soothe our dry, cracked, irritated souls in the living water that only God can give. As we draw closer and deepen our relationship with him, living water flows in us so that we shall never thirst again (vv. 13–14).

Prayer: *Loving God, help us to tap into the living water that only you can offer. Amen*

Thought for the day: Our relationship with God can satisfy and refresh us.

Karolyn Miller (Tennessee, US)

In Unison

Read Ecclesiastes 4:9–12
'This is how everyone will know that you are my disciples, when you love each other.'
John 13:35 (CEB)

My family and I visited a theme park that features Clydesdale horses. Out in the pasture, they are magnificent, beautiful animals. And when they are working as a team to pull large wagons throughout the parks, it is truly a wonder to behold.

Just as the Clydesdales are bound together with a harness and trained to work in unison to pull heavy loads, so Christians are bound together by the love of Christ. We are called to show 'compassion, kindness, humility, gentleness and patience' (Colossians 3:12). When we forgive as God has forgiven us, we allow peace to rule our hearts (see Matthew 6:12; Ephesians 4:32; Colossians 3:13). We can worship God by working together to accomplish the work placed in our path. Much like the team of Clydesdales pulling the wagon, we can work in unison to complete God's mission for the world.

Prayer: *Dear God, help us to act in ways that show those around us our compassion, kindness, gentleness and patience. Amen*

Thought for the day: We can have unity when we love Christ and make his desires our desires.

Mike Slaton (Alabama, US)

PRAYER FOCUS: THOSE WHO CARE FOR ANIMALS

Not Weary?

Read Romans 12:4–12
Those who wait for the Lord shall renew their strength, they shall mount up with wings like eagles, they shall run and not be weary, they shall walk and not faint.
Isaiah 40:31 (NRSV)

Everyone told me that getting into one of the best medical schools in Puerto Rico would not be easy. Even though I was a good student and had faith in God, I had my doubts when I applied. I knew the competition would be difficult.

I remember the day I was accepted. My father handed me the big envelope containing the letter, which began with 'Congratulations'. My father and I cried and fell to our knees, giving thanks to God. I would be the first doctor in my family. But I still had to face many challenges. In my first year, I was at the point of failing my anatomy class. At the end of my second year, I had to postpone my final exams due to incomplete course work, which then delayed the start of my third year.

Through these struggles, I have learned to rely on God. As I begin my third year, I now truly understand that those who wait on the Lord will gain new strength, that with each new challenge I can rise like the eagles. In spite of the difficulties I can walk and not grow weary because the Lord will always be by my side to protect and guide me.

Prayer: *Dear God, thank you for walking with us in every situation. Guide us and grant us peace. Amen*

Thought for the day: Each new challenge can renew my faith in God.

Dalimar Panell Diáz (Puerto Rico)

Time Well Spent

Read Ruth 1:11–17

Do not cast me off in the time of old age; do not forsake me when my strength is spent.
Psalm 71:9 (NRSV)

Recently, I attended church services with two of my friends who are elderly. Afterwards, when they invited me to lunch, I politely accepted, although it wasn't my idea of fun. After lunch, I was invited to help conduct an afternoon church service at a retirement home. This was not how I had imagined spending the last few hours of my weekend. I wanted to entertain myself with a film, a trip to the shops or a cup of coffee with a friend. But, I felt obligated to go to the retirement home. However, once I arrived, my attitude quickly changed. I had interesting conversations, shared hugs and watched the eyes of these older saints light up with joy, like those of young children on Christmas morning.

My Sunday afternoon at the retirement home reminded me of Ruth and how her commitment to her mother-in-law, Naomi, has always inspired me to be a better person. Then I realised for the first time that on one level, Ruth's story is about cherishing the elderly.

When we honour older people by spending quality time with them, we show them that they are valuable, and in the process we honour God. And whenever we honour God, we walk through a doorway of unexpected riches—just like Ruth did.

Prayer: *Dear God, guide us in choosing where, when and with whom we will spend our time so that we can best share your boundless love with others. Amen*

Thought for the day: One of God's greatest gifts is time to spend with others.

Kenneth Avon White (Tennessee, US)

Gratitude Stone

Read Ephesians 5:15–21

Give thanks in every situation because this is God's will for you in Christ Jesus.
1 Thessalonians 5:18 (CEB)

Every day I put a stone in my pocket or wallet. It was given to me by my spiritual mentor and serves as a reminder not to let a day pass by without thanking God.

One hot afternoon, I was distributing letters by car with another church member. We were on our way to our final destination, when traffic trapped us for almost half an hour. I became impatient and complained about how long it was taking. But my companion smiled and said, 'Taking public transport would take us longer than driving.' His words woke me up, and I remembered the stone in my pocket.

Most of the time, we see what's missing in our lives rather than what we have. We complain more than we give thanks. In 1 Thessalonians 5:18 we read that we are to 'give thanks in every situation', even in difficult circumstances.

Instead of fuming about the traffic, I should have said, 'Thank you, God.' We can find a symbol or recall a verse of scripture to remind us to give thanks to God in every situation. Such a practice can help us turn complaints into words of gratitude.

Prayer: *Dear Lord, teach us to utter words of thanks each day. Amen*

Thought for the day: Giving thanks to God is better than complaining.

Sharamae I. Cea (Quezon, Philippines)

Well Equipped

Read 2 Timothy 3:14–17

All Scripture is God-breathed and is useful for teaching rebuking, correcting and training in righteousness so that the servant of God may be thoroughly equipped for every good work.
2 Timothy 3:16–17 (NIV)

An ancient proverb states, 'An unbalanced load will not reach its destination.' My two oldest children and I learned this truth the hard way while on a camping trip in Tajikistan. We had hastily loaded our gear on the backs of several donkeys, a common mode of travel in this part of the world. The unbalanced load caused one of our donkeys to stumble, endangering the animal and spilling our gear all over the steep mountain track. We struggled on our journey because we had failed to prepare well.

As I reflected on the proverb and my experience in the mountains that day, I was reminded that good preparation is essential in my spiritual journey as well. When we carefully study God's word, we are properly equipped for the journeys of our days. Consistently immersing ourselves in scripture and prayer is time well spent.

Prayer: *Dear God, stir up within us a deeper hunger to read and study your word, so that we may be properly equipped for your service. As Jesus taught us, we pray, 'Our Father in heaven, hallowed be your name, your kingdom come, your will be done, on earth as it is in heaven. Give us today our daily bread. And forgive us our debts, as we also have forgiven our debtors. And lead us not into temptation, but deliver us from the evil one.'* Amen*

Thought for the day: How can I share my delight in God's word today?

Timothy Austin (Istanbul, Turkey)

PRAYER FOCUS: TO ENSURE I MAKE TIME FOR BIBLE STUDY
* Matthew 6:9–13 (NIV)

The Lodgepole Pine

Read John 12:24–26

I am about to do a new thing; now it springs forth, do you not perceive it?
Isaiah 43:19 (NRSV)

On a recent trip to South Dakota and Wyoming I learned about the lodgepole pine, a tree native to the area. One of its unusual characteristics is its serotinous cone, which means that it releases its seeds when exposed to extreme heat. This results in the propagation of new trees after a forest fire. When told about this, I marvelled at the intricacy of God's creation, which has a plan designed to sustain life in the midst of destruction.

We sometimes experience 'forest fires' of tragedy and suffering in our lives, resulting from forces outside ourselves and sometimes from our own sin. In the midst of these events in our lives, it can be difficult to see how God will bring good from the situation. The prophet Jeremiah wrote, 'Surely I know the plans I have for you, says the Lord, plans for your welfare and not for harm, to give you a future with hope' (Jeremiah 29:11). I know from personal experience that we often feel God's love and healing most powerfully in difficult situations. In all circumstances, God can bring transformation and new life.

Prayer: *Creator God, we trust you to be with us in all life's circumstances because you have a plan for our welfare. Help us to trust you in life's difficult times, knowing that you can bring good out of everything that happens to us. Amen*

Thought for the day: God brings new life and healing.

Karen E. Brown (Mississippi, US)

Our Great Fortress

Read Psalm 62:1–8

Truly my soul finds rest in God; my salvation comes from him. Truly he is my rock and my salvation; he is my fortress, I will never be shaken.
Psalm 62:1–2 (NIV)

The children's hospital was quiet in the early morning hours, except for the murmurs from the nurses' station down the hall and the consistent beeping of machines throughout the ward. Fervently, I prayed the words of the psalmist quoted above as chemotherapy did its work within my body.

This was a time of profound pain, confusion and fear for me. But from this scripture I called out to God and, quicker than a breath, the Great Comforter filled me with a sense of peace.

Though the seas grow strong, though the winds grow violent, and though our footing may falter, we can always find refuge in God's arms. Regardless of our circumstances, our suffering and pain, one truth remains: God is our fortress; we will never be shaken!

Prayer: *Dear Father, may our eyes never leave your beauty. You alone are all that we need. Amen*

Thought for the day: Today I will remember the faithfulness of God.

David Hughes (Australian Capital Territory, Australia)

Walking with a Guided Heart

Our predecessors in the faith knew that prayer embeds biblical revelation and activates it in our lives. So, *lectio divina** was never merely an act of reading; it is prayerful reading—reading with an open heart in the spirit of an ancient prayer, 'Give me a word that I may live.' We search for a word of life—a word that leads us from being wanderers to being pilgrims, from darkness to light... *Lectio divina* is a form of prayer that begins, runs through and ends the entire reading process.

This discovery transformed me. Reading the Bible has always served as my primary means for growing as a Christian. In fact, I could (and still can) get lost in scripture. The reading alone had negatively affected my devotional life; I would plan a time to both read and pray, only to realise I had spent all the time reading. My prayer life suffered as I tried to rush through a list of intercessions far too fast and superficially. I found the endeavour frustrating.

And then I learned that early Christians and many others since have never separated reading and praying. From the moment they opened the Bible, they were praying. Since prayer is always a response to God, what better time to pray than while we listen to God's voice in scripture? As soon as we turn to the Bible reading for the day, we are receivers from the God who speaks and shows divine truth to us, and who, in that revelation, invites us to enter the text and give ourselves to it. Once I understood this invitation, my devotional life changed. I no longer compartmentalised or categorised. All was prayer—prayer in response to scripture and then prayer in relation to life situations. From start to finish—prayer!

Lectio divina produces the spirit of attentiveness. Rather than reading quantitatively, I began to read qualitatively. The Bible has the potential to change us with a single word or verse. While we can make good use of suggested reading plans, the point of reading scripture is not to follow a plan but to discover a Person.

Lectio released me to see that even though I might read a prescribed amount each day, I did not have to do so. I could freely choose to stop, look and listen whenever prompted by the Spirit. I could read deeply, not just broadly. Words and phrases came alive in this kind of reading because I gave myself permission to pay attention to them rather than feeling obligated to complete a certain amount of content. I had no daily-reading box to check, so my reading became more relaxed. *Lectio* gave me an attentiveness for the word.

Lectio also produced a spirit of engagement. Set free from the more-is-better approach, I could dig into those words and ideas that struck me, spoke to my mind or warmed my heart. I did not have to move on. I could walk around a passage, spend time with it and savour it. I could bring forth previous knowledge I had about the passage and make use of resources that would shed new light upon it. Using this approach, I began to see the multiple layers of biblical meaning. In terms of discernment, this engagement revealed that praying to know God's will requires an unhurried embrace of the message. God wants to guide us through the whispers of grace (the nuances), not just the shouts (big-picture insights). *Lectio* created a disposition of the heart to pay attention to scripture and to look for the God-word in the word of God.

Questions for Reflection

1. What methods or practices do you use to help you read scripture attentively?

2. Which Bible passages have helped you to listen for God's guidance in your life?

* Also called 'praying the scriptures,' *Lectio Divina* is a slow, meditative reading and reflection on a passage of scripture. For more information, go to: http://prayer-center.upperroom.org/resources/resources-articles/49

Dr Steve Harper is a retired elder in the United Methodist Church and a retired professor. He has been married to Jeannie for over 40 years, and they have two children and three grandchildren. This prayer workshop was adapted from his book *Walking in the Light: Knowing And Doing God's Will* (Upper Room, 2014).

A Legacy of Faith

Read Ephesians 1:3–8

Because of the Lord's great love we are not consumed, for his compassions never fail. They are new every morning; great is your faithfulness.
Lamentations 3:22–23 (NIV)

My earliest and fondest memories of childhood are of waking and going to find my mother. She was usually sitting in her room reading her Bible. Upon finding her, I would jump into her lap and she would continue reading with me. On one of these mornings I first saw *The Upper Room*, which my mother used as her devotional reading for many decades.

After years of rebellion in college, I came to know Christ more deeply through the copies of *The Upper Room* that my mother would send me from time to time. I began to have a deeper connection with God, starting each day with it.

God does not change, but our understanding of him changes and grows. Our daily faith practices help our understanding of God to grow, and they give us new perspectives on life. These activities become the foundation for a meaningful relationship with God that guides me each day.

Today my children do what I did with my mother. They come early in the morning, climb on to my lap, and listen as I read *The Upper Room*. Life has come full circle.

Prayer: *Guide of humanity, thank you for knowing us, loving us and pursuing us long before we recognise our need for you. Amen*

Thought for the day: God's grace has no limits or conditions.

Mathew A. Palakunnathu Punalor (Kerala, India)

Going God's Way

Read Proverbs 16:1–9

*'My thoughts are not your thoughts, neither are your ways my ways,'
declares the Lord.*
Isaiah 55:8 (NIV)

One beautiful November morning, I decided to tackle the leaves in my garden. The day was pleasant outside but breezy. I started up the leaf blower. I soon discovered that even though I wanted to blow the leaves due north, a north-west wind was blowing the leaves back behind me into the areas I had cleared. I realised that to be productive, I needed to change my strategy and blow the leaves more toward the east, in the direction the wind was blowing. Once I did that, my job was much easier, since I was using the wind to my advantage instead of fighting it.

Then I remembered Isaiah 55:8, in which God says, 'My thoughts are not your thoughts, neither are your ways my ways.' How many times have I tried to do things my way and not God's way? How often, when I insisted on doing things my way, did the results blow back into my face, like the leaves in the wind that morning? But I have found that my progress is not hindered when I decide to listen to God's words and to follow his ways.

Prayer: *Thank you, Lord, for reminding us that we can trust you for guidance. Amen*

Thought for the day: God shows us the way; all we need to do is follow.

Peg Foltz (Illinois, US)

Programmed for Faithfulness

Read Psalm 1:1–6

Blessed is the one… whose delight is in the law of the Lord, and who meditates on his law day and night. That person is like a tree planted by streams of water, which yields its fruit in season, and whose leaf does not wither—whatever they do prospers.
Psalm 1:1–3 (NIV)

Our world changed dramatically with the invention of computers. They have revolutionised how we work and how we play. They are in our cars, toys, appliances, aeroplanes, home security systems and phones. For computers to function, they need detailed instructions: a blueprint called a computer program. A well-crafted computer program enables the device to perform specific tasks successfully.

I think the Bible acts like a computer program in our minds and hearts, enabling us to live faithfully. When we read and think about scripture, the Holy Spirit begins to enlighten us. As we spend time soaking in God's truth, it begins to transform us, enabling us to understand and obey God's word. If we are meditating on a scripture that highlights God's love, for instance, the Holy Spirit can help us to comprehend the goodness of the Lord and to treat others with kindness. When we choose to make God's word our focus, we can be programmed for leading fulfilling spiritual lives.

Prayer: *Dear God, thank you for scripture. Give us understanding and help us to put your word into practice. Amen*

Thought for the day: Meditating on God's word programs our lives for faithfulness.

Tom Toya (Illinois, US)

What Do You Want Me to Do?

Read Mark 10:46–52

Jesus said to [Bartimaeus], 'What do you want me to do for you?'
Mark 10:51 (NRSV)

Jesus is walking along the dusty road when he hears loud shouting. 'Son of David, have mercy on me,' comes the repeated plea. Jesus stops and calls for the blind man to come to him. It seems obvious what he needs, but Jesus still asks him, 'What do you want me to do for you?' Only after Bartimaeus expresses his deep longing to be healed does Jesus restore his sight.

Often I do exactly what Bartimaeus did. I pray in vague terms, asking God to 'bless' my family or 'pour out mercy' on my country. But since taking time to reflect on this passage, I have been trying to pray in more specific ways. Recently I was a speaker at a devotional-writing workshop hosted by Africa Upper Room Ministries. I normally get very nervous when I speak to a crowd, so I was worried that my voice would shake or that I would forget everything I had so carefully prepared to say. I asked God to take away all my anxiety as I stood up to speak. Only when I looked back over the morning did I realise that I had not had a single moment of nervousness. My request wasn't as big as the one Bartimaeus made, but God still faithfully answered my specific prayer.

The story of Bartimaeus encourages us to bring all our requests to God, no matter how big or small they may be.

Prayer: *Dear God, thank you for your love, faithfulness and willingness to be involved in each of our lives. Amen*

Thought for the day: Today I will pray for a specific need.

Joan Campbell (Gauteng, South Africa)

The Bud of New Life

Read 1 Peter 1:3–8

Each of you should use whatever gift you have received to serve others.
1 Peter 4:10 (NIV)

When I belonged to the local rose-growing club, I learned that most rose varieties are developed by grafting a bud-eye of the desired variety onto a rootstock. Whatever bud-eye the gardener grafts onto the rootstock will determine the characteristics of the new bush.

I see a spiritual parallel to this. When we become part of God's family, the wild part of us is cut off and a new life is grafted onto our 'rootstock'. Just as the gardener determines what kind of rose he or she will propagate, God determines what spiritual gifts we will have to minister to others in the body of Christ.

One of the hardest things for me to accept is that God didn't give me the spiritual gifts that I used to think I wanted—gifts that would make me stand out as a 'spiritual celebrity'. Instead, I find myself doing what anybody could do: giving out groceries at a food bank, making sandwiches for a homeless shelter, or writing words of encouragement to grieving friends. From my experience over the years, I have concluded that God is not as concerned with gifts that bring us personal recognition as with those we can use to help meet the needs of others.

Prayer: *Dear Father, help us to stop wishing for spiritual gifts we don't have and instead to embrace the ones you have given us and use them to minister to others. Amen*

Thought for the day: How can I use my gifts to serve others?

David Bonner Smith (Oregon, US)

The Source of Courage

Read Philippians 1:20–26

God didn't give us a spirit that is timid but one that is powerful, loving and self-controlled.
2 Timothy 1:7 (CEB)

After my stroke, I wanted to get better and return to my family and the life I had left. But after seven months I had made minimal progress; I couldn't move or talk.

When I finally got home—in my wheelchair—everything was in place for my care. I thought that this would be how I would live for the rest of my life. I would never be able to care for myself fully again. I felt as if someone had kicked me in the stomach.

The people who visited me told me how strong I was for having gone through so much. But I didn't think of myself as particularly strong; thousands had done it before me. They even said I had courage. Me, courageous?

A few years went by, before I began to realise that I wasn't fighting this 'courageous' battle alone. God had been with me all along. When I look back at those early days, I recall I would often feel a sense of calm when I was scared. Where did that come from? I believe God was telling me that everything would be all right.

Every day I continue to deal with the effects of my stroke. But every day God is here keeping me going—giving me courage and helping me to inspire others.

Prayer: *O God, when we find ourselves fighting for health, even for our very lives, we thank you that you fight with us. Encourage us with your love shown to us by those who join in our struggle. Amen*

Thought for the day: Courage comes from faith that faces fear.

Gail Babula (New Jersey, US)

Ungodly Assumptions

Read James 4:11–12

Who are you to judge your neighbour?
James 4:12 (NIV)

One summer, during my daily walks, I saw a middle-aged couple scurrying to their cars each morning. The man carried a lunch box; I assumed he was going to work. The woman hustled to get two small children in the child seats of her car; I assumed she was the children's grandmother.

Often she looked unhappy. I wondered if she wanted to take care of the children. Why couldn't the children's parents take care of them? Did the children's parents care that this early morning routine might be difficult for the grandparents? I was quick to think unkindly of those parents whom I had never even seen.

After a few months, I no longer saw the couple, but I learned that their daughter was dying that summer. That's why the grandparents were caring for the children. How wrong I had been! Now I was filled with compassion for the family.

From this experience, I learned first-hand the meaning of Jesus' question in Matthew 7:3: 'Why do you see the speck in your neighbour's eye, but do not notice the log in your own eye?' (NRSV). Only God knows what is in our hearts and what is happening in our lives. Remembering this, we can treat our neighbours with greater compassion.

Prayer: *Dear God, help us to look at our neighbours with compassion, not judgement. Amen*

Thought for the day: I will treat others with compassion and leave judgement to God.

Catherine A. Welch (Connecticut, US)

Prayers during Persecution

Read Acts 12:1–11

Blessed are you when people revile you and persecute you and utter all kinds of evil against you falsely on my account. Rejoice and be glad, for your reward is great in heaven, for in the same way they persecuted the prophets who were before you.

Matthew 5:11–12 (NRSV)

Reading about modern-day martyrs has prompted me to pray every day for countries in the world where it is dangerous to be a follower of Jesus. I read about a young girl whose mother threatened to kill her if she accepted Jesus. A young Christian couple who sought to marry received a 15-year prison sentence. Trying to escape, the woman was beaten at the airport and then assaulted by police. The couple is in hiding now.

  Situations like these drive me to my knees in prayer for all people who are seeking God—especially those facing circumstances like the ones described above. I have decided to pray for each country in the world over the course of each year. Accordingly, I select a country for each day of the week. Then I pray for God to bless each of those countries. For any country that is hostile to Christianity, I pray that God will raise up individuals who will introduce Christ to their people. I pray that scripture will be made available in more languages and for volunteers who will devote themselves to learning those languages to be able to go and teach. My hope is that the next generation who lives in those countries will learn about Jesus and live by his principles.

Prayer: *Defender of the helpless, console and strengthen those who suffer for their faith in you. In Jesus' name we pray. Amen*

Thought for the day: Today I will remember Christians who are suffering for their faith.

Andy Baker (Tennessee, US)

Dogged Devotion

Read Psalm 46:4–11

Cast all your anxiety on [God] because he cares for you.

1 Peter 5:7 (NRSV)

When my wife and I pray together before going to bed, our dog, Bubu, always jumps up on the settee next to us. He does this because he wants to get closer to us. As we start to pray, he puts his head on my wife's lap, and before we say 'Amen', he's asleep. With dogged devotion, he does this every night.

Bubu's desire to be near us has taught me something about prayer. Often while praying, I focus only on what I am asking God to do for me—not on what his presence means to me. At times I cannot fully experience the benefit of the apostle Peter's advice when he wrote, 'Cast all your anxiety on [God] because he cares for you' (1 Peter 5:7). It seems that I am so focused on casting my anxiety on God that I pay little attention to the part of the verse that says, 'because he cares for you'. Now, each time I pray, I remember to focus on God and the power of his loving presence to calm my worries and fear.

Prayer: *Dear God, help us to remember that being with you is just as important as what we are asking of you. We pray in the way that Jesus taught us, saying, 'Our Father in heaven, hallowed be your name, your kingdom come, your will be done, on earth as it is in heaven. Give us today our daily bread. And forgive us our debts, as we also have forgiven our debtors. And lead us not into temptation, but deliver us from the evil one.'* Amen*

Thought for the day: In prayer, I will focus less on needs and requests and more on basking in God's presence.

Aristotle S. Garcia (Bataan, Philippines)

* Matthew 6:9–13 (NIV)

Abide with Me

Read Matthew 25:31–40

'I was sick and you took care of me.'
Matthew 25:36 (NRSV)

Doug, who looked after our community gardens, was dying of cancer. I wrote to him while he was in hospital, thinking that would be the one and only time I would do so. I didn't really know Doug but wanted to give him some support.

Imagine my surprise when, a week later, I received a response from him. His letter included one of his poems along with a book of stamps. I knew when I got that book of stamps that he hoped I would keep writing. I wrote to Doug every seven to ten days but never received another response. I became a carer from a distance. I don't know why Doug picked me to be his correspondent, but I felt honoured to be chosen. I felt that I was abiding with him during those last four months of his life.

I was blessed to be able to show God's love and care to Doug during that time. I'm glad I paid attention to the prompting to reach out to him. We never know when Christ will call us to be his hands and feet. It's up to us to be awake, to listen and then to respond.

Prayer: *Thank you, loving God, for the opportunities you give us to serve others. Amen*

Thought for the day: Today I will listen for God calling me to serve others.

Barbara Michael (Missouri, US)

Escaping Bitterness

Read 2 Corinthians 2:5–10

Be angry but do not sin; do not let the sun go down on your anger.
Ephesians 4:26 (NRSV)

I went to college with a dream of creating television and film entertainment. When I left, the few local television shows and one film I worked on did not lead to additional projects. Over time my dream has melted away, but a recent opportunity offered me a second chance. I worked for months to make the most of this opportunity, but then my business partner told me that he was no longer interested. I felt angry, betrayed and bitter.

That same week my church group studied forgiveness. We read Proverbs 20:22 and discussed biblical ways of working through a wrong done to us. We read Mark 11:25 where we are instructed to forgive offences before we pray. I thought that to be able to forgive, I had to find a way to get past my bitterness. The only solution I could think of was to pray that God would change me. Over time those prayers helped me move beyond my bitterness and anger.

God can free us from these and other emotions that destroy our joy and keep us from forgiving others. We can always rest, knowing that God is just a prayer away to help us change.

Prayer: *Dear God, comfort us in times of hurt and disappointment. Lead us into your word where we can find strength, direction and renewed hope. Amen*

Thought for the day: Reading scripture can direct us to new ways of living.

Avon White (Tennessee, US)

Knots

Read James 3:9–18
A gentle word turns away wrath, but a harsh word stirs up anger.
Proverbs 15:1 (NIV)

My family and friends enjoy the scarves I knit for them. I try to find the softest yarn in wonderful colours to make their gifts. The yarn comes in twisted skeins but needs to be rolled into balls to prevent tangles. Sometimes as I roll it, the yarn still seems to tangle. If I tug hard on the tangle, it creates a knot that is almost impossible to remove. But if I am gentle, taking care to notice what's causing the problem, the potential knots almost untangle themselves.

Sometimes my relationships also seem to tangle without cause, all but closing off communication with the people I care about. I have to remember in that moment the words from Proverbs: 'A gentle answer turns away wrath, but a harsh word stirs up anger.'

So when I have been offended by someone I care about, I try to slow down and look at that 'tangle' as a potential 'knot' in our relationship. That keeps me from answering with harsh words or an angry tone of voice.

How we respond in hurtful situations makes a difference in our connection with other people and with God. When we heed the words of Proverbs 15:1, we give our relationships a better chance to flourish and to enrich our lives.

Prayer: *Dear Lord, help us to model your loving-kindness in our responses to others. Put a guard on our mouths so that we don't hurt others or ourselves. Amen*

Thought for the day: With God's help I can speak blessings to others.

Pamela Gilsenan (Colorado, US)

The Noble Ones

Read Mark 2:1–12

I say of the holy people who are in the land, 'They are the noble ones in whom is all my delight."
Psalm 16:3 (NIV)

The four friends of the paralysed man in today's reading would not allow any barriers to stand between them and bringing their friend to Jesus. They were so determined that they dug a hole in the roof of the house where Jesus was preaching. I believe their efforts in bringing their friend to the Lord were only a small part of the time they must have invested in him. Who clothed and fed him? Who helped him relieve himself and cleaned up after him? Who provided a place for him to stay? Were these men his carers? No doubt his life was not only in their hands but on their hearts.

For the seven months I was struggling with cancer, I called my wife my cellmate. Our lives had come to a standstill, but she didn't complain. She cared for me and informed our family and friends of my progress. I'm sure I would not be where I am today if not for those who kept me on their hearts.

If anyone deserves to be honoured today, it is those who serve unnoticed in caring for those who are ill or disabled. Though they are forgotten by many, to those they care for they are like the psalmist's noble ones in whom he delighted.

Prayer: *God of all compassion, thank you for those who unselfishly serve those who are sick or disabled. Bless them with your love and care. Amen*

Thought for the day: When we give our hearts to God, our hands will follow.

Mark Weinrich (Nevada, US)

Well Pleased

Read Matthew 17:1–13

While [Peter] was still speaking, a bright cloud covered them, and a voice from the cloud said, 'This is my Son, whom I love; with him I am well pleased. Listen to him!'
Matthew 17:5 (NIV)

When I watch my sons perform in a concert or represent their school in playing sport, I'm overcome with emotion. I often get nervous before the event. I get tearful and excited when they perform well and grieve when they fail. If they succeed, I'm flooded with pride afterwards. I'm not used to such strong emotions and the feeling that I have little control over them.

My response to these events makes me wonder whether God feels the same way about us. We are told that we are made in the image of God, and the New Testament tells us that he was 'well pleased' with Jesus as a son. It is extraordinary to think that God might look at something I'm doing and have the same strong emotions that I experience as a parent.

Meditating on the image of God being well pleased with Jesus encourages me that, just as my children bring me joy, my ordinary life may bring joy to my heavenly Father.

Prayer: *Dear Lord, help us to find fulfilment in the knowledge that you love us. Amen*

Thought for the day: God delights in us.

Wendy Marshall (Tokyo, Japan)

Let it Snow

Read Isaiah 55:8–13

As the rain and the snow come down from heaven, and do not return to it without watering the earth and making it bud and flourish... so is my word that goes out from my mouth: it will not return to me empty, but will accomplish what I desire and achieve the purpose for which I sent it.
Isaiah 55:10–11 (NIV)

For me, one of winter's greatest pleasures is to go for a walk in a gentle snowfall. The air is cold and crisp, and my footsteps make a soft, muffled sound. The snow is beautiful, but it also serves a purpose. Snow that falls heavy on the fields and mountaintops refills the depleted water reserves below the ground. Then the land and all that lives on it grows and is refreshed. The excess snow melts into streams and rivers, which flow to the seas, where water evaporates and goes back up to the heavens to start the cycle again.

Such is God's word to our hearts and minds. When we read the Bible, it may apply to our lives at the moment or it may not soak in immediately but remain in our hearts until a new season. As it cycles through our lives, it brings growth and refreshment to our souls.

Prayer: *Dear God, as we read your word, let us learn from it and let it soak into our hearts so that we feel refreshed in you. Amen*

Thought for the day: The words of scripture refresh our hearts.

Karen S. Weaver (Ohio, US)

What Weeds?

Read Mark 4:3–20

Those sown among the thorns… are the ones who hear the word, but the cares of the world, and the lure of wealth, and the desire for other things come in and choke the word, and it yields nothing.
Mark 4:18–19 (NRSV)

I enjoy gardening and love to share the fruits of my labour with neighbours and friends. My least favourite task, however, is keeping up with annoying weeds. Left unattended, they choke off otherwise healthy plants, reducing the harvest. I have to take the time to pull or dig out the weeds, making sure to get the roots out so that they don't grow back again.

Weeding my garden reminds me how easy it is to allow 'weeds' to grow my spiritual life. Distractions, negativity and temptations can quickly grow deep roots. When they are left unattended, they prevent us from bearing spiritual fruit. Jesus' parable of the sower teaches us not to let 'the cares of the world, and the lure of wealth, and the desire for other things come in and choke the word'. It takes work to keep the 'weeds' out of our daily lives. But with diligence, we can put distractions behind us and replace them with Christ's love. We can then share the love of Christ with everyone we meet.

Prayer: *Dear Lord, help us to rid our lives of distractions and fill our thoughts and hearts with your love. Amen*

Thought for the day: What do I need to uproot from my life to be more fruitful for God?

Ray Appel (Wisconsin, US)

God's Place for Me

Read Ephesians 4:11–16

We are God's handiwork, created in Christ Jesus to do good works, which God prepared in advance for us to do.
Ephesians 2:10 (NIV)

When I went to visit Maria, I found a clean and tidy house that smelled of freshly baked bread. Everything was ready for her husband and three sons to return home from work and school. But Maria wasn't happy.

'The sermon on Sunday was about using our talents,' she said, 'but I don't feel I have any. I married very soon after leaving school and when the children came along I couldn't continue my small job in the office. These days I never manage to tell anyone about Jesus and his love.' I assured Maria that she displays the love of Jesus to others every day. Her sons have always brought their friends over to spend time in a home where they have always felt loved and welcomed. Besides these acts of hospitality, Maria has supported her husband in his many different activities. Furthermore, she is a compassionate listener for her neighbours and serves in the church in many ways. She is the biblical Martha and Mary—all rolled into one.

The mission field for some of us is abroad; for others it's the home, office, church or neighbourhood. Wherever we serve God and our neighbours is the place where God needs us to be.

Prayer: *Loving God, help us to serve enthusiastically in the situations where you have placed us. Amen*

Thought for the day: God has placed me precisely where I can serve best.

Carol Purves (Cumbria, England)

Hospitality to Strangers

Read Hebrews 13:1–3

Do not forget to show hospitality to strangers, for by so doing some people have shown hospitality to angels without knowing it.
Hebrews 13:2 (NIV)

A weary traveller, I emerged from the metro car in Paris after a very long flight. I struggled with the two large pieces of luggage I had brought with me. An escalator surely must be nearby. But as I turned the corner, I sighed and dropped my bags. The escalator was out of order. Rush hour was just beginning and hundreds of Parisians passed me by, hurrying to their destinations, never even noticing, perhaps even irritated, that I had stopped and was in their way. Suddenly I felt someone reaching for the bag on my right. When I realised the woman was reaching not to steal my bag but to carry it for me, I grabbed the other bag and together we made the long trek.

The Good Samaritan was a young Muslim woman wearing a hijab. When we reached the tree-lined avenue outside the metro station, she left my bag and proceeded on her way. All I could do was yell, 'Shukran!' the Arabic word for 'thank you'.

This woman saw my need and met it. Her action reminded me that no matter who we are, where we come from or the basis of our faith, in the end we are all God's children. Her kindness inspired me to show hospitality to friends and strangers alike.

Prayer: *Dear God, help us to exercise our privilege of service to meet the needs of all your children. Amen*

Thought for the day: Today I will offer hospitality to strangers in my path.

Teresa Cannady (Florida, US)

God's Masterpiece

Read Psalm 19:1–8

Heaven is declaring God's glory; the sky is proclaiming his handiwork.
Psalm 19:1 (CEB)

One weekend my college hiking club decided to go camping in the mountains near a well-known spectacular view. We were hurriedly setting up tents before it got dark when someone noticed a glow in the sky just beyond the ridge top. We dropped everything and raced up the hill. There, we saw spread out before us one blue ridge after another, disappearing into the distance. The sky was a brilliant mix of pink and orange. Everyone was silent, stunned by the beauty.

As I stood there, I agreed with the psalmist's words in the verse quoted above. The magnificent scene in the heavens made my heart yearn to praise God and to express my gratitude for creation. Whenever we explore the grandeur of the world around us, we can delight in God's creative power. Every breathtaking sight reminds us to pause and give thanks.

When we feel helpless in the face of challenges of life, we can look at creation and know that just as long ago God made the splendour around us from a world that was void and empty, he is still creating magnificent masterpieces. Knowing that God can also make our lives beautiful, we can celebrate the beauty of creation.

Prayer: *Dear God, thank you for the wonderful world you created. May the glory of your creation always remind us that you are still creating a glorious life within each of us. Amen*

Thought for the day: Where have I seen God today?

Kevin Main (Florida, US)

PRAYER FOCUS: HIKERS

The Storm

Read Luke 8:22–25

Who then is this, that he commands even the winds and the water, and they obey him?
Luke 8:25 (NRSV)

I lay in bed listening to the wind roaring around the house, wondering what damage it would do. Our TV screens revealed the devastation the next morning, with powerful waves lashing the coast, rivers overflowing into houses and streets and the Somerset Levels engulfing farms and cutting off whole communities. People's lives were thrown into chaos as they had to evacuate their homes and their livelihoods were threatened.

Storms were a common occurrence on the Sea of Galilee. Perhaps the storm in today's reading was more powerful than the disciples, even though they were fishermen, had ever experienced. The powerful waves were threatening to sink the boat, and they were afraid.

Jesus was fast asleep in the boat, oblivious to the storm, until he was disturbed by the frantic cries of the disciples. Couldn't he see that they were about to perish?

Jesus woke and immediately stilled the storm. 'Where is your faith?' he asked them.

At times we all experience the storms of life, which can batter our faith and trust in God. But Jesus says that it is precisely when things are tough that we should trust him, stop and listen to his voice.

Prayer: *Dear Lord, help us to know that you are with us in the storms of life. Amen*

Thought for the day: To trust in the Lord no matter what life throws at us.

Anne Rasmussen (Somerset, England)

Made Clean

Read Hebrews 10:19–24

Repent… and turn to God, so that your sins may be wiped out, that times of refreshing may come from the Lord.
Acts 3:19 (NIV)

In our busy home, laundry tends to pile up, and in a rush to finish the washing I tend to omit important steps in the cleaning process—like pre-treatment of stains. I cross my fingers in the hope that the stains will simply disappear during the washing process. It's most frustrating when some persistent ones remain and I have to put the item of clothing back in the wash.

In a similar way, the stains in my soul may be difficult to deal with. How often do I simply brush off my transgressions? I forget about the unkind words that have left my mouth or the overdue apology. Maybe I have hurt someone badly and simply swept the incident under the carpet. Sometimes my sin may be more serious, seemingly unforgivable. At these times, my relationship with God is affected.

But there is hope. No matter what our personal blemishes are, we can have confidence that ours is a God of amazing grace. Jesus' death on the cross offers us the opportunity to come clean and to be forgiven. We can start again with a spotless new life and a wholesome relationship with our heavenly Father.

Prayer: *Thank you, merciful God, that we are able to come before you, confess our sins, and receive forgiveness. Thank you for the new and clean life that you offer to each of us. Amen*

Thought for the day: Christ's sacrifice has taken away the stain of my sin and washed me clean.

Caryl Moll (Gauteng, South Africa)

You Answered

Read 2 Samuel 22:7–20

'In my distress I called out to the Lord… From his temple he heard my voice… He brought me out into a spacious place; he rescued me.'
2 Samuel 22:7, 20 (NIV)

I can still remember the day a tornado developed just minutes away from my house. Even though it was small, its presence was shocking because Central Pennsylvania is not the typical place for tornadoes, big or small. I can still remember praying as the wind howled and the thunder clapped. I had never been so frightened.

Later, I remembered the words of today's reading—that David began by telling us of his distress and ended with a description of God's rescue.

When we call out to God, we can trust that he will answer. In times of trials, tribulation and even tornadoes, God is present with us. He will not forsake us but will lead us through the storm. As the sky grows dark and storm clouds roll in, he does not leave us. No matter what the circumstances or situation, when we call, God answers.

Prayer: *Help us, O Lord, to remember that you are with us always. Give us the assurance that if we call you will answer. As Jesus taught us, we pray, 'Father, hallowed be your name, your kingdom come. Give us each day our daily bread. Forgive us our sins, for we also forgive everyone who sins against us. And lead us not into temptation.'* Amen*

Thought for the day: In the next trial or tribulation I face, I will call to the Lord.

Ryan M. Arndt (Pennsylvania, US)

PRAYER FOCUS: THOSE EXPERIENCING STORMS
* Luke 11:2–4 (NIV)

Time with Mum

Read Psalm 71:15–18
Those who have been replanted in the Lord's house… will bear fruit even when old and grey… they will remain lush and fresh in order to proclaim… 'The Lord is righteous. He's my rock. There's nothing unrighteous in him.'
Psalm 92:13–15 (CEB)

What can we do today? I thought as I arrived at the nursing home. Mum could no longer concentrate on television programmes or find hidden words in word-search puzzles. Her confusion made conversation difficult.

I looked at her snoring softly in the armchair, next to the table. Her brown, worn Bible sat there with some of her other personal possessions. I had not read a Bible in months but opened it to the book of Psalms and began to read aloud. When I glanced back at my mother, she opened her eyes and smiled at me. 'Thank you,' she whispered.

The following morning, I once again found the Bible and I read to her, this time from the New Testament. Reading her Bible aloud became a daily routine until she passed away at the age of 97.

My mother's simple gratitude encouraged me to continue reading to her, which led me back to a faith I had lost. And I was reminded that God is with me all the time. Now, I see my mother's face in my mind each morning when I pick up my own Bible.

Prayer: *Dear God, thank you for older people. Help us take time to listen and learn from them. May we find ways to be a source of comfort to them in their later years. Amen*

Thought for the day: God's word can reach us when nothing else can.

Nancy Shelton (Missouri, US)

Mighty Warrior

Read Judges 6:11–16
The angel of the Lord appeared to [Gideon] and said to him, 'The Lord is with you, you mighty warrior.'
Judges 6:12 (NRSV)

When God called me to lead our congregation, I was afraid. It is one thing to help the minister and quite another to take on that role myself. When I read the stories of God's people I want to be like David, walking out against Goliath, but often I behave like Saul when he hid among the baggage (see 1 Samuel 10:22). I would like to leave everything without hesitation and follow Christ as his first disciples did, but instead I make excuses, as Moses did when God called him to lead the Israelites out of Egypt.

Not long after I accepted the challenge to become a minister, one brother in Christ advised me to read the story of Gideon, the judge of Israel. The more I read this story, the more I recognised myself in Gideon's response: fear, doubt, uncertainty, questions and cowardice. Yet God's messenger addressed Gideon as 'mighty warrior' (Judges 6:12). God did not seem to be interested in how strong, clever or experienced Gideon was.

From Gideon's story, I conclude that God doesn't require us to be completely equipped to serve from the beginning. Instead he can use weak, insignificant, foolish and cowardly folk like us so that all the power and glory belong only to him.

Prayer: *All-powerful God, may your strength be revealed in our weakness, your wisdom in our folly and your boldness in our fear. Amen*

Thought for the day: When I am serving God, my fear can become the fuel for action.

Vladimir Ditmar (Kirov, Russia)

Rejoice!

Read Psalm 42:1–5

Rejoice in the Lord always. I will say it again: Rejoice!

Philippians 4:4 (NIV)

At the age of 23 our son contracted a mysterious illness; his condition baffled the doctors. After two-and-a-half months with no hope for his recovery, we released our child from life support. That first week after our son's death our church family passed around an old Bible and asked members to underline a favourite scripture passage. When we received the Bible, I was struggling even to pray. But I was able to cling to those verses shared by our church friends. Someone had highlighted Paul's words to the Philippians, 'Rejoice in the Lord always.' At first, I felt the verse inappropriate for our situation. What did we have to rejoice about? But the scriptures repeat again and again that we should praise God in all things.

I began to give thanks for what I could—the air we breathe, the sun in the morning and the rain in its season. My praise sounded false at first, but with practice I repeated my thanks. Miraculously, over time, I was filled with Christ's peace—the peace that transcends understanding (see Philippians 4:7). Through scripture and the simple act of thanksgiving, God can give us a balm for anxiety, stress, depression and grief.

Prayer: *Dear Lord, we thank you for the healing that praise can bring. Give us the strength to glorify you in all situations. Amen*

Thought for the day: Practising gratitude can lead to renewed faith.

Chris Baldauf (Louisiana, US)

'Wow!'

Read Psalm 104:24–34
Pray continually.
1 Thessalonians 5:17 (NIV)

When I was a young Christian, I understood 1 Thessalonians 5:17 literally: we should spend every moment speaking to God. I was puzzled by the thought of praying continually, 24 hours a day, seven days a week. At that time, I found prayer illusive; it did not satisfy the need I had for a deeper relationship with God. Prayer seemed to be a one-way conversation. I talked; God listened, but did not participate. Reading and discussing the subject led me in many directions, but the words of my prayers still seemed to bounce off the ceiling.

Then on a solo nine-day canoe trip through the Florida Everglades, I looked up at the sky and saw a sunset spilling onto the surface of the still water. It was the third day of the trip, and I had not encountered another human being. So I was startled to hear my own voice utter aloud, 'Wow!' It was my shortest and perhaps my most honest prayer. Now I understand that an appropriate offering to God is gratitude not just in words, but as deep appreciation for a flower, a landscape, another human being, a perfect mathematical equation, music that reaches deep down into my being—all of creation.

Prayer: *Dear God, create in me a grateful heart. Amen*

Thought for the day: Deep gratitude is always an appropriate prayer.

Bill Roy (Florida, US)

Waiting in Wonder

Read Isaiah 11:1–9

Come, Lord Jesus!
Revelation 22:20 (NRSV)

When I was a boy, my parents would get an Advent calendar for my brother and me each year. The calendar was special for us because it was filled with chocolates in the shapes of angels, stars and Christmas trees. Each day in December as we looked toward Christmas, we would open a window in the calendar and eat a piece of chocolate. The whole month of December is already filled with reminders to cause any child to burst with anticipation of the big day—the decorations, the ever-present music, the gifts beginning to appear under the Christmas tree. Yet somehow the daily chocolate from the Advent calendar had a way of capturing that expectation in a special way.

Advent is to Christmas what Lent is to Easter. As one carol says, it is a time to 'let every heart prepare him room'. During Lent we look to take on a spirit of repentance. During Advent we wait for One who brings what we need, personally and globally—peace within and peace for the world. When we contemplate everything Jesus represents, a child's sense of anticipation and wonder at Christmas is more than fitting.

Prayer: *Help us, God, to be like a child in our anticipation of your renewed presence in our lives this Christmas. Amen*

Thought for the day: Joy to the world! The Lord is come!

Joel Boon (Minnesota, US)

Generation after Generation

Read Psalm 78:1–4

I am reminded of your sincere faith, which first lived in your grandmother Lois and in your mother Eunice and, I am persuaded, now lives in you also.
2 Timothy 1:5 (NIV)

I asked my sister if she knew how long our mother had read *no Cenaculo* (the Portuguese edition of *The Upper Room*). Her answer was, 'Always.' She remembered that when we were children we always had prayers before going to bed. One family member read the Bible passage; the prayer and thought for the day were read by someone else and repeated by all of us together. Then one of us led our prayer time. I miss that time and remember it with joy. Proverbs 22:6 was taken seriously by my parents: 'Start children off on the way they should go, and even when they are old they will not turn from it.'

My mother worked as a distributor for this magazine for many decades. With the struggles of ageing, she handed the responsibility to a niece, who was honoured to take over the task. My family has delivered this devotional guide one generation after another. I have a habit of cutting out some pages and handing them out to people: petrol station attendants, shop assistants and cooks at my school. When I don't take any pages with me, people ask, 'Where is that little paper?'

I enjoy sharing my faith and spreading the joy that *no Cenaculo* has brought my family for many generations.

Prayer: *Loving God, we thank you for the opportunity to know you. Bless all those who contribute to* The Upper Room *and those who will read it. In the name of Jesus Christ. Amen*

Thought for the day: With whom will I share my faith story today?

Joeli Grimbos Marques Souza (Parana, Brazil)

First Sunday of Advent

Read Matthew 1:18–25

[Mary] will bear a son, and you are to name him Jesus, for he will save his people from their sins.
Matthew 1:21 (NRSV)

It was Christmas week, and I had to lead the Christmas services. My 18-year-old son was supposed to go with me, but that night in his quiet hospital room I had learned that his broken neck had developed an infection, and that his quadriplegia was permanent. When Christmas carol singers came down the hall singing, 'We wish you a merry Christmas!' and 'Deck the halls with boughs of holly', I closed the door. How could any grieving person celebrate Christmas with such cheery songs?

Later, I stood at the dark window staring through the fog at the dim, coloured lights across the way. Then I felt God saying to me, 'On that first Christmas there were no pretty lights adorning the streets of Bethlehem, no carol singers on the roads, no pretty presents around the stable. In the midst of a world of so much darkness and despair, your Saviour came as a helpless baby in a manger, to love you back to wholeness.'

The prophet Micah wrote, 'You, O Bethlehem… are only a small village… Yet a ruler of Israel will come from you' (Micah 5:1–2, NLT). That ruler—Christ the Lord—will save his people. Christmas is for those who have no joy and no home—for all those who have lost their way. Surely that Christmas was for my son and me.

Prayer: *Holy God, bless us and comfort us according to our need. Amen*

Thought for the day: We can celebrate God's gift of Jesus with both silence and singing.

George Nye (Oregon, US)

God is Always There for Us

Read Psalm 23

We know that in all things God works for the good of those who love him.
Romans 8:28 (NIV)

A biologist once told me that it was a good thing that spiders were not sociable creatures, like bees, as their huge number would soon enable them to take over the world! Science also informs us that the fine thread spun by a spider is actually stronger than steel drawn out to the same thickness.

Last winter, my husband and I went for a morning walk across a nearby field. There had been a hard frost during the night and to our amazement and delight the wild, rough tussocks of grass were covered in wonderful spiders' webs. The whole field looked as though it had delicate lace spread over it. By the time we returned that way, however, the sun had melted the frost and the webs had disappeared, though they were still there; we just could not see them.

This made me reflect that sometimes the pattern of our life is upset. Something difficult or distressing happens and we can't recognise the hand of our heavenly Father in our circumstances. At another time, a happy series of 'coincidences' seems to confirm that God is at work. I believe that whether it is clear to us or not, God is always there for us, making sense of our lives, creating a beautiful pattern which we will see one day, if not now. I think we can pray for the grace to glimpse what he is doing and for the faith to trust him when we cannot see the pattern.

Prayer: *Lord, help us to trust that you are always at work in our lives, especially when times are tough. Amen*

Thought for the day: Today I will look for signs of God's presence in my life.

Hazel Fitz-Gibbon (Surrey, England)

Be the Light

Read John 1:1–9

No one after lighting a lamp puts it under the bushel basket, but on the lampstand, and it gives light to all in the house.
Matthew 5:15 (NRSV)

At our kitchen table, I was watching a candle in the process of burning out. Its wick burned too low and would soon be below the level of the wax. Then the flame would die. At the same time I remembered two candles among our stored Christmas decorations. They were still brand new, though they were purchased several years before. Our mum always enjoyed them as a focal point of her living room decorations at Christmas. But she never allowed anyone to light them. They never fulfilled their chief purpose.

We Christians can be like that. We can tell all about the Bible. We can articulate our belief on this or that aspect of faith. But when we don't get around to putting our faith into action, we are like a candle left unlit. Our faith is shallow. Like a lamp lit and put under a bushel, we fail to share Christ's light and hope and to fulfil Christ's command for us to tend to the least and the lost (see Matthew 25:40).

In every season of life we can find a new commitment to be Jesus' hands and feet, serving those in need whenever and wherever God may bring them across our path.

Prayer: *O God, help us to find a new vision of the reason you sent Jesus into our world. Help us to bring him into our world again in faith, in word and in action. Amen*

Thought for the day: How will I let my light shine today?

Floyd Twilley (Maryland, US)

A Lesson from My Inbox

Read 1 Corinthians 9:24–27
Indeed we call blessed those who showed endurance.
James 5:11 (NRSV)

Another prayer request arrived by email, and I was feeling overwhelmed. My women's group emailed prayer requests regularly, and another urgent need from a parishioner wrenched my heart. How would I find time to add another intercessory prayer to my already lengthy list, while giving each the depth and fervour it deserved?

As I was pondering, another email from a long-time friend popped into my inbox. She wanted me to know she had prayed for my strength and endurance to do the ministries the Lord had given me. She mentioned how grateful she was for the prayers and spiritual comfort I had offered her through the years. I was surprised and humbled by how much my actions meant to her.

Suddenly my prayer list seemed manageable. And I realised that I did not need to place particular time limits on my prayers. Physical problems have somewhat curtailed what I can do to serve the Lord, but I am able to pray for others here at home. My friend's email had served as the encouragement I needed to persevere.

Prayer: *Dear Lord, help us to pray with open, honest, loving hearts for the intercessions with which you have entrusted us. Amen*

Thought for the day: Whom can I encourage to persevere in prayer?

Gael Stuart Phaneuf (Colorado, US)

Rescued

Read Psalm 18:16–19

He reached down from on high and took hold of me; he drew me out of deep waters.'
Psalm 18:16 (NIV)

During our college days in Northern California, my friends and I decided to go for a swim in the turbulent waters of the Pacific Ocean. One place in particular was called 'the bowl'. Rightly named, it's a place where the waves slam into the rocky cliffs and create a whirlpool of surging, foaming seawater. The waters were especially unsettled that day. Four of us jumped in, but a few moments later only three emerged. I could not manage to grab hold of the rocks to pull myself out. With the water tugging me under, I was losing strength quickly and beginning to panic. Then I saw my friend reaching down from the rocks above me. Managing to take hold of his hand, I allowed him to pull me up to safety. As I sat on the shore catching my breath, I thanked God for sending help.

When we find ourselves in situations that threaten our physical, spiritual or emotional well-being, we can be tempted to despair. If we're not careful, we can miss the help God is sending our way. A timely message, a scripture verse, someone to listen, the prayers of a friend—even the outstretched arm of a friend to pull us out of the water—are just a few of the ways God can come to our aid.

Prayer: *Dear God, when we are tempted to lose heart, remind us to look to you and receive the help you so lovingly offer. Amen*

Thought for the day: We can call on God for help when we feel powerless.

Timothy Austin (Turkey)

PRAYER FOCUS: SEARCH-AND-RESCUE WORKERS

Experiencing God's Love

Read 1 Peter 1:3–9

See what love the Father has given us, that we should be called children of God; and that is what we are.

1 John 3:1 (NRSV)

My son's football team has not won any games this season. Each time they play, they get better but not good enough to defeat their opponents. I was unable to attend one of their games, but another mother took pictures and sent them to me. The next day when I was looking at the pictures, I noticed that one picture showed the boys and coaches in prayer. The next one showed the team celebrating with their hands in the air and smiles on their faces. I thought these pictures must have been taken before the game because the team had lost 8–1. But a member of the team told me the pictures had been taken after the game. I asked, 'Why are you so happy?' He replied, 'First, we thanked God for a safe and fun game. After the prayer, our coach told us, "Never lose your passion, no matter what the outcome", and we just felt like celebrating!'

God loves us and wants us to experience joy, love and victory. We can find something to celebrate even in circumstances that may dictate otherwise. By doing so, we experience the love of God. No matter what life hands us, we can stay strong in our faith and never forget that God is with us.

Prayer: *Dear Jesus, thank you for loving us. Help us to look for you in every situation so that we can experience your love in all we do. In Jesus' name we pray. Amen*

Thought for the day: Today I will celebrate God's love, no matter what happens.

Leasa Hodges (North Carolina, US)

Open Hearts

Read Philippians 4:4–8

I pray that… Christ may dwell in your hearts through faith, as you are being rooted and grounded in love.'
Ephesians 3:16–17 (NRSV)

I said goodbye and hung up the phone with a smile after another long conversation with my daughter. We share every detail of our lives during these talks. There's no point in either of us trying to hide anything because the other would sense something was wrong before the call ended. We know each other so well.

It wasn't always this way. For several years we hardly communicated, despite our mutual love. As a result we felt unsure where we stood, and rare, stilted exchanges became the norm. I didn't want to call and bother her over something trivial.

For some of us, time spent with Christ follows the pattern my daughter and I used to have. We neglect prayer, widening the distance between ourselves and the Lord, and the intimacy of our relationship suffers. We begin to think Jesus doesn't care about us, doesn't want to waste time on us. But nothing could be further from the truth. God wants us to pray without ceasing (see 1 Thessalonians 5:17) and never tires of us or the mundane details of our lives. Just like in my conversations with my daughter, the more I pray, the easier it becomes to open my soul to God. We can trust the Lord with our secrets, our pain and our shame. He loves us more than anyone else ever has or ever will.

Prayer: *Dear Lord, as we pray to you, help us feel your presence and your love. Give us the ability to perceive your answers. Amen*

Thought for the day: God is always ready for a conversation with me.

Heidi Gaul (Oregon, US)

PRAYER FOCUS: ESTRANGED FAMILY MEMBERS

Second Sunday of Advent

Read Romans 8:26–31

We know that in all things God works for the good of those who love him, who have been called according to his purpose.
Romans 8:28 (NIV)

During my wife's pregnancy we took time to prepare in great detail for the birth of our first daughter. We devoted time to choosing her name, the nursery decor and the baby clothes. We wanted to be sure to record every detail of her birth.

After seven and a half months of peaceful pregnancy, however, the doctor discovered a problem. We were rushed to the hospital. Maria Eduarda was born a few hours later and taken to the intensive care unit. And while still in the delivery room, my wife and I were told that our daughter had Down's syndrome. Our dreams and preparations were rocked. We grieved the loss of our idealised baby.

The days in the intensive care unit were hard. In the midst of our anxiety and suffering we called out to God, and he answered our prayers. Today Maria Eduarda is healthy—delighting everyone with her charisma, wit and strength.

When things don't turn out the way we plan, we can become frustrated and scared. But if we devote ourselves to living faithfully, acknowledging that God is with us, we will be uplifted and strengthened. God's care for us is real and everlasting in any circumstance life brings.

Prayer: *Loving Father, forgive us when we feel the need to be in control and forget that you are guiding our way. Thank you for caring for us during troubling times. Amen*

Thought for the day: God can bring new life out of any situation.

César Eduardo Lavoura Romao (Sao Paulo, Brazil)

First Impressions

Read James 2:1–5

'Judge not according to the appearance, but judge righteous judgement.'
John 7:24 (KJV)

Each week when our pastor tells the congregation to take out their Bibles, my husband takes out his smartphone. This has earned him more than one raised eyebrow or disapproving glance from those seated nearby.

If they looked closer, however, they would see that he, too, is opening his Bible—via an application on his phone. This comes in handy, as he can go quickly to the verse he needs, and he can also highlight passages, look up related devotional material and study guides, view maps and bookmark favourite verses. In addition, he knows whenever he has his phone with him, he has his Bible, too.

At first I felt a little angry with those so quick to judge based on what they thought they were seeing. But then I remembered that I too have been hasty to run with a first impression often based on unimportant factors such as how people are dressed, how they talk or their mood at the time.

In 1 Samuel 16:7, we are reminded that God 'looks on the heart' (NRSV). Perhaps if we took the time to look a little closer at those we judge on first impressions, we might better be able to do just that.

Prayer: *Dear God, helps us to 'look on the heart' when we see others and not focus only on outward appearances. Amen*

Thought for the day: 'The Lord looks on the heart' (1 Samuel 16:7).

Lisa Kay Tate (New Mexico, US)

God's Calm

Read Psalm 121:1–8
God is our refuge and strength, a very present help in trouble.
Psalm 46:1 (NRSV)

While I was driving in a remote area, the right front wheel of my car hit a chunk of concrete. The force of the impact flattened the tyre and bent the wheel's rim. I was unable to drive the car, and I could not get a mobile signal to call for help. Feeling helpless and uncertain, I thought of the Israelites in the wilderness. God provided food and water for them when none was available. Could I count on God to provide the help I needed? I recalled the verse quoted above as well as Psalm 121:2: 'My help comes from the Lord, who made heaven and earth.'

When I prayed to God for help, I found myself calming down and thinking more clearly. I flagged down a delivery truck and asked if I could use the driver's phone. Help came, and I thanked God.

Whenever we feel trapped in a hopeless situation, praying can bring help—first by calming us down so that we can think and see clearly. This may help us to see other ways to solve our problems or other sources of help. Given time and patience, the problems may resolve themselves. Instead of giving in to panic, we can ask God for the insights or answers we need to deal with the situation.

Prayer: *Dear Lord, help us to trust you to guide us when we have problems. In Jesus' name, we pray. Amen*

Thought for the day: When problems arise, we can start to face them by praying.

Gerald Bauer (Ohio, US)

Spiritual Lives

Read Hebrews 12:1–3

Just as you received Christ Jesus as Lord, continue to live your lives in him, rooted and built up in him, strengthened in the faith as you were taught, and overflowing with thankfulness.
Colossians 2:6–7 (NIV)

My friend and I enclose letters with our yearly Christmas cards. When I opened Cindy's card this year, I was eager to hear of her latest family activities. Her chatty letter began, 'How is your spiritual life?' What an odd way to start a letter! I always write, 'How are you?' And Cindy had always done so in the past. Her new question made me wonder if she didn't care about physical health: I have multiple sclerosis and my husband, Kurt, has brain cancer. Her question annoyed me.

However, as the New Year approached, I pondered which was more important: our physical health or the health of our spiritual lives? Of course, I immediately knew the answer: the condition of our spiritual lives. God knows my spiritual life and how I'm doing.

But Cindy's question made me realise that I need to be more aware of my spiritual life. Do I read my Bible daily and spend time with other Christians? Does my love for God show in my words and actions? Are my thoughts fixed on Jesus? Do I remember to thank God as well as making requests? These and other concerns will lead each of us to greater spiritual health.

Prayer: *Lord God, help us remember to examine our spiritual lives each day to make sure we are living for you. Amen*

Thought for the day: How is my spiritual life?

Sue Carloni (Wisconsin, US)

Summer Camp

Read Ephesians 4:29—5:2

Peter came to Jesus and asked, 'Lord, how many times shall I forgive my brother or sister who sins against me? Up to seven times?' Jesus answered, 'I tell you, not seven times, but seventy-seven times.'
Matthew 18:21–22 (NIV)

Last month I helped my grandmother at a summer camp where she was a teacher. One day, three young campers were involved in an argument. One of the girls was insulting the other two. Following the argument, the girls did not speak to each other. But after a while, the girl who insulted the others admitted her guilt and apologised to the other girls. They embraced and carried on as before.

After observing that incident, I gained a new perspective on forgiveness. At times we become angry with our neighbour and tempers flare. But at the end of the day, it is right to swallow our pride and ask for forgiveness. God grants us forgiveness every day. How can we withhold forgiveness from one another?

Prayer: *Eternal Father, we are grateful for your mercy. Help us to show mercy to our neighbour as we pray, 'Our Father which art in heaven, Hallowed be thy name. Thy kingdom come. Thy will be done, as in heaven, so in earth. Give us day by day our daily bread. And forgive us our sins; for we also forgive every one that is indebted to us. And lead us not into temptation; but deliver us from evil.'* Amen*

Thought for the day: Whom do I need to forgive today?

Nicole González Rodriguez (Puerto Rico)

Sharing God's Goodness

Read Hebrews 13:16–21

Do not forget to do good and to share with others, for with such sacrifices God is pleased.

Hebrews 13:16 (NIV)

Many years ago, a former student called at my office with a Christmas gift. As she handed it to me, she smiled and thanked me for the study tips I had given her during the term. Because I knew that she and her family often struggled to pay for her tuition and other college costs, I had not expected a gift from her. I opened the bag and pulled out the gifts: an apple, an orange and some sweets. The student said that she wanted to buy something more expensive but that these gifts were all she could afford. I received several other gifts that Christmas, but I have always remembered this former student's generosity.

Just as the young woman shared with me, God gives us opportunities to share and is pleased when we extend kindness to others. Today we can reach out to people in simple ways—a phone call, a hug or a kind word. By doing good and sharing with others, we show our gratitude for God's love and mercy.

Prayer: *Dear Lord, teach me how to share your love with others. Amen*

Thought for the day: Today I will look for ways to share God's love.

James C. Hendrix (Indiana, US)

'Who Am I to Do This?'

Read Exodus 3:1–12

Those who hope in the Lord will renew their strength. They will soar on wings like eagles; they will run and not grow weary, they will walk and not be faint.
Isaiah 40:31 (NIV)

Some of the most beautiful sunrises and sunsets I have ever seen have occurred while I was standing on an aircraft carrier in the middle of the ocean. In quiet moments like those, I can sometimes sense God speaking to me and calling me to do something. Unfortunately, my response is often similar to Moses': 'Who am I to do this? Surely others are more qualified!' But God's answer is simple: 'I didn't ask them. I asked you.' I see now that many of the great heroes of the Bible doubted or hesitated at God's call. What made them great was not their abundant self-confidence but their faith in God.

At times, we may feel unable or unqualified to do what God is asking of us. We may respond by turning away in fear or denial. But instead of ignoring God's call, we can stop and think about his answer to Moses: 'I will be with you' (Exodus 3:12). If we can be certain of God's presence with us, if we can have as much faith in him as he seems to have in us, then we can boldly pursue whatever is asked of us.

Prayer: *Our Father in heaven, help us to have the unshakeable faith that we can do whatever you have asked of us. Amen*

Thought for the day: When God doesn't call the qualified, he qualifies the called.

Jason Ponzio (Georgia, US)

Third Sunday of Advent

Read Deuteronomy 6:1–9

Keep these words that I am commanding you today in your heart. Recite them to your children and talk about them when you are at home and when you are away, when you lie down and when you rise.

Deuteronomy 6:6–7 (NRSV)

At Christmas our family sits down together to watch the Christmas films and cartoons we have collected over the years. We also give one another presents and play various games. The celebration of Christ's birth is particularly special for me. I always wait impatiently for Christmas and rejoice when it comes.

When I was a child we didn't celebrate Christmas. I knew nothing about this celebration until the fall of Communism. Then everything changed. Missionaries started to come and they told me about Jesus. I remember my first Christmas; I was a student at a technical college.

How joyful I am that our children can celebrate this wonderful holiday and that their memories of Christmas will take them back to their childhood! Three generations of people had to live without Christmas when Christianity was banned from my country. But today we can celebrate freely. We have the responsibility to pass on our faith and the joy of Christmas to those who come after us.

Prayer: *Dear Lord, we thank you that we can celebrate Christmas. Help us to greet the day of your birth with joy and carry this celebration to those places where people know nothing of the good news of your Son. Amen*

Thought for the day: In what new way can my family celebrate Christ's birth this year?

Evgenii Tarasov (Moscow, Russia)

PRAYER FOCUS: CHRISTIANS WHO CANNOT CELEBRATE OPENLY

Praying for My Enemies

Read Matthew 5:43–48

Jesus said, 'I tell you, love your enemies and pray for those who persecute you.'

Matthew 5:44 (NIV)

One afternoon I received an email that I thought was from our bank. In a rush, I replied with the requested security information and fell victim to identity theft. We immediately changed our passwords, cancelled our credit cards and did everything we possibly could to ensure that the scammer could not get into our accounts. Nevertheless, four days later I received a call from a bank—a woman claiming to be me was trying to open a credit card account and make a large purchase at a store. As I continued to get calls from stores and banks where this woman was trying to impersonate me, I couldn't even find the words to pray. My husband encouraged me to pray David's words from Psalm 140:8, 'Do not grant the wicked their desires, Lord.'

As I prayed, I also began to think about this woman. What kind of brokenness had led her to become a thief? Because Jesus told us to pray for our enemies, I began praying that God would use my connection with this woman, which had begun in darkness, to bring light into her life (see John 1:5).

This experience has opened my heart to understand what it means to pray for our enemies. Through prayer we work with God to bring light to the world.

Prayer: *Dear Father, help us to pray for those who have hurt us. Thank you for shining the light of salvation into the world. Amen*

Thought for the day: Praying for someone who has hurt me can bring both of us new life.

Jennifer Parra (Texas, US)

Great Joy

Read Luke 1:46–55

When [the wise men] saw the star, they rejoiced with exceeding great joy.
Matthew 2:10 (KJV)

When Mary learned that she would bear a child, she sang, 'My spirit rejoices in God my Saviour' (Luke 1:47, NRSV). When the shepherds found the Christ child, they returned to their fields 'glorifying and praising God' (Luke 2:20, NRSV). When the Magi found Jesus, 'they rejoiced with exceeding great joy' (Matthew 2:10, KJV).

When we grasp the truth of Christmas, we find amazing joy: a long-lasting, life-energising, soul-strengthening, heart-warming joy. Jesus came to show us what God is like. He worked continually for our good and even died for us. God will do whatever it takes to reach us. That is the truth of Christmas.

When we see the Christ child as the expression of God's love for us, we find joy that flows from the steadfast love of God. We may find entertainment or escape at the shopping centre, but we find joy at the manger.

Prayer: *O God, give us the great joy of those who have found the Christ child. Amen*

Thought for the day: Jesus is our picture of God's unfailing, self-giving love.

James A. Harnish (Florida, US)

Reflected Light

Read Matthew 5:13–16
You are the light of the world.
Matthew 5:14 (NRSV)

During the Christmas season, my custom has been to draw back the curtains in my living room, switch on the Christmas tree lights so that they shine out in the half-light of early morning, and read my daily *Upper Room* meditation. One morning last Christmas, I opened the curtains but neglected to switch on the tree lights. As I finished reading the meditation, I looked up and saw that in the gloom was a bright light, shining from the tree. I stood up to look more closely, only to realise that the light from my reading lamp was being reflected by a multifaceted tree ornament.

Then, I thought of the words of Jesus: 'Let your light shine before people, so they can see the good things you do and praise your Father who is in heaven' (Matthew 5:16, CEB).

I asked myself what qualities I needed to reflect to those I meet day by day. As that Christmas ornament has many facets, I too reflect a variety of attitudes: false pride, arrogance, selfishness, boastfulness—mixed up with more worthy attitudes of helpfulness, kindness, compassion, love and service. By daily spending time with God, I pray that my better characteristics will shine more brightly on others.

Prayer: *Dear Lord, may the people we meet see your love reflected in our attitudes and actions. Amen*

Thought for the day: God calls us to reflect love and compassion to the world.

Brian Beeson (Derbyshire, England)

PRAYER FOCUS: SOMEONE WHO NEEDS A KIND WORD FROM ME

Overcoming through Endurance

Read John 16:28–33

'He that overcometh… shall be clothed in white raiment; and I will… confess his name before my Father, and before his angels.'
Revelation 3:5 (KJV)

My friend Lisa taught me that overcoming sometimes means enduring. As a young mother she learned she had cancer. She battled the disease for nearly ten years, all the time refusing to allow her illness to control her life. Despite the pain she endured, she remained faithful to God. I learned from Lisa that to overcome doesn't require that we achieve healing or fully understand our situation. Overcoming can mean persevering in the face of adversity, standing strong in convictions and beliefs.

The Bible tells us about many of God's people who stood firm in the face of danger. When God told Abraham to move to an unknown land, Abraham obeyed (see Genesis 12), later becoming the father of a great nation. Joseph remained faithful to God through trial after trial and ended up in a position of power from which he could rescue his people (see Genesis 37—47). Rahab risked her life to hide Israelite spies (see Joshua 2—6) and became an ancestor of Christ (see Matthew 1). All had faith in God's promises. Today, people continue to know God through these stories. All through the ages, God has been faithful. He walks with us in our struggles and provides all we need to endure.

Prayer: *Protector of all who trust you, thank you for your promise to be with us always. No matter what happens, you have overcome the world! Amen*

Thought for the day: With God's help, I can persevere in the face of adversity.

Shelley Pierce (Tennessee, US)

PRAYER FOCUS: CANCER PATIENTS

A Mother's Heart

Read Luke 1:46–56

The Lord himself goes before you and will be with you; he will never leave you nor forsake you. Do not be afraid; do not be discouraged.
Deuteronomy 31:8 (NRSV)

Many years ago when I was seven months pregnant with my fourth child, we had to move to a new city. My daughter was born one week before Christmas—far away from family, friends and trusted doctors.

As I was studying the Bible that Advent season, I felt a deeper understanding of Mary's circumstances. My pregnancy was unexpected like Mary's, but no suspicion surrounded my baby's paternity. I travelled comfortably by car to our new home. I knew my baby would be born in a clean hospital with trained doctors, and I had already experienced other labours and deliveries. Yet I had been consumed with fear and anxiety about this relocation and the impending birth. I have to wonder what the very young Mary was thinking. What were her fears? Did she question God's timing? All we see in scripture is Mary's absolute trust: 'I am the Lord's servant,' Mary said. 'May your word to me be fulfilled' (Luke 1:38, NIV).

Scripture tells us that we cannot always expect to understand God's wisdom (see Isaiah 55:9). But we can always aspire to Mary's profound faith and trust in God.

Prayer: *Dear Lord, when we allow fears and anxieties to crowd our minds, help us to deepen our faith and to trust your amazing love. Amen*

Thought for the day: As I face today's challenges, I will seek to show Mary's unwavering faith.

Debbi Whitezell (Pennsylvania, US)

Emmanuel—God with Us

Read Psalm 98:1–9

Jesus said, 'I myself will be with you every day until the end of this present age.'

Matthew 28:20 (CEB)

One early morning, I was out walking in the quiet and peaceful countryside. After the first turn on my walk, I came across a shady patch of road where the breeze was gentle and soothing and fragrant. A little further on, I saw a wisteria bush bearing four sprigs of blossoms—fragile and delicate—in exquisite shades of purple. Around another turn, I heard the distant laughing call of kookaburras. Whenever I hear these birds, it seems to me that God is sharing a joke with whoever chooses to listen.

When I turned back, the three-quarter moon caught my eye. It was high in the western sky and shone brightly in the blue of the early-morning heavens.

Four things had caught my attention. None was of great importance by itself, but I saw in them a message from God that Jesus—Emmanuel—brought to the world: 'I am with you in the big things and in the little things. At every twist and turn of life, I am there!'

Prayer: *Loving Father, help us to notice you in what is going on around us. Amen*

Thought for the day: What is God showing me today?

Meg Mangan (New South Wales, Australia)

Fourth Sunday of Advent

Read 1 John 4:7–16

God has given us eternal life, and this life is in his Son. Whoever has the Son has life; whoever does not have the Son of God does not have life.
1 John 5:11–12 (NIV)

A friend of mine was unpacking the nativity set that came out every year to be a central figure in her Christmas decorations. As she carefully unwrapped each figure, she was shocked to find that baby Jesus was missing. She stared mesmerised at the empty space in the familiar scene. Panic set in. Frantically she removed all the packaging to search in the bottom corners of the box. There he was! What an enormous relief.

Later, she found herself thinking, 'What if that were reality? What if Jesus had never come?' and a sense of desolation swept over her. We would never have Christmas. We would never have known the love of God, the gift of salvation, the forgiveness of our sins or the presence of our risen Lord day by day. Then she looked at the figure of Jesus in her nativity scene, and was overwhelmed with gratitude and joy. Jesus did come and live as one of us; he gave his life for us that we might receive eternal life; he was raised from the dead and lives for ever; he promised to be with us always. What a transformation he brings. What a Saviour; what a loving God!

Prayer: *Thank you, Lord Jesus, that because you came as a baby to Bethlehem we have life, joy and hope. Amen*

Thought for the day: Give thanks to God for all the blessings we receive through his Son.

Hazel Thompson (Somerset, England)

That is Enough

Read 2 Corinthians 4:16–18

Even though our outer nature is wasting away, our inner nature is being renewed day by day.

2 Corinthians 4:16 (NRSV)

I feel very blessed to have a job where each day the first order of business is Bible reading. I am an activities manager at a care home for senior citizens. We have a group of about 15 'regulars', who range in age from 80 to 100 years of age. We always read the daily meditation from *The Upper Room*, and I make a point of reading the writer's name and location. I think this makes the members of our group feel that they are a part of a much larger community of believers, many of whom are dealing with similar feelings and problems in remote parts of the globe. We often give thanks to God that we live in a country where we can practise our faith openly and without fear of censorship or oppression. We are also saddened to know that many people in our world do not have the freedom to profess their Christian faith openly.

The words of the apostle Paul above remind us that we still have a purpose in life even though our abilities might be limited by age and disease. Even if the only thing we can do to help in any given situation is to pray, that is enough.

Prayer: *Faithful God, thank you for our worldwide Christian community. Help us to find ways to serve you wherever we are. Amen*

Thought for the day: At every stage of my life, God has work for me to do.

Becky Duke (Pennsylvania, US)

The Family of God

Read John 3:1–17

God so loved the world that he gave his one and only Son, that whoever believes in him shall not perish but have eternal life.
John 3:16 (NIV)

From the time I was a child, I have never experienced the fullness of love from my family. My mother and father didn't relate to each other well, nor did my mother and grandmother. As children, my twin sister and I tried not to be a burden on our family. I sensed that my parents wanted me to become independent as quickly as possible so that they could be free from the burden of having to look after me. At that time in my life, I could never have believed that there might be anyone who would be concerned about me.

When I was 33 years old, I came to know Jesus through a Korean friend. Then, at 34 when I became part of a church, I found that loving family I had never known before. There I heard the words, 'I love you' from an American friend and the word 'saranheyo', which in Korean also means 'I love you.' I had never heard these words spoken to me before. My heart was full!

I am even more amazed by the love God expresses for us every day—even at this very moment. Along with my brothers and sisters in the faith, I have found the love I had been missing. With them, I pray that we will be able to share God's love with those who do not know it.

Prayer: *Our Father, we thank you that you have made us your family through your grace shown in Jesus. Help us to love you more deeply each day as we also love others. Amen*

Thought for the day: God is loving me at this very moment.

Misako Hatano (Nagasaki, Japan)

A Gift Given

Read Matthew 2:1–11

[The Magi] saw the child with his mother Mary, and they bowed down and worshipped him. Then they opened their treasures and presented him with gifts.
Matthew 2:11 (NIV)

I vividly remember one day close to Christmas when a friend called with a Christmas gift for me. Unfortunately, I did not have one to give in return. I had already purchased all my Christmas gifts, and she had not been on my list. I awkwardly invited her in and opened the gift. I thanked her, we talked and she left with empty hands.

While she was still there, I tried to work out a way I could wrap something I already had. After she had left, I wanted to run out to the nearest shop and pick out something as nice as her gift, if not better. Just then, an internal voice reminded me of how much my situation was similar to what we all encounter in God's gift that we receive and celebrate at Christmas.

We can never repay God's gift of Christ. Often we try to make it up to God by doing good deeds, regularly attending church and seeking to grow spiritually. Sometimes we feel so unworthy that we resist God's grace. But in the end we realise that a gift is a gift. Gifts do not demand repayment; they are freely given out of love. All we can do is accept God's gift with joy, and then allow that gift—Jesus Christ—to become a part of who we are.

Prayer: *Dear God, may we freely receive the greatest gift ever with thanksgiving and love. Amen*

Thought for the day: What does the gift of the Christ child mean to me?

Tim Tate (Virginia, US)

Grace Abounds

Read Genesis 15:1–7

The one who started a good work in you will stay with you to complete the job by the day of Christ Jesus.
Philippians 1:6 (CEB)

Abram remained childless for many years after God first promised to make of him a great nation. During that time, he gave in to fear while in Egypt, lying about his wife and putting her in potential danger. Later, quarrels arose between his people and his nephew Lot's people. Abram was even forced to battle several nomadic kings. And still no child was born to Sarai.

Abram may have thought that he no longer deserved the promise and that he would never receive the blessing. But then the Lord appeared again to Abram and told him to get out of his tent and look into the night sky. I think God was telling Abram to let go of the limitations of the man-made tent—what Abram's hands could accomplish—and come out into God's expanse. Under the night sky, God renewed the promise made to Abram. The troubles of Abram's life did not hinder God's ability to make the promise of descendants a reality. Abram would yet experience the grace of God in his life.

Our scars and brokenness do not limit God from working in our lives. His grace toward us abounds.

Prayer: *Thank you, loving God, that your grace is enough to cover our past, present and future. Amen*

Thought for the day: God's grace never ends.

Rhett Wilson (South Carolina, US)

Christmas Day

Read Luke 2:8–20

This will be a sign to you: You will find a baby wrapped in cloths and lying in a manger.
Luke 2:12 (NIV)

The young African girl froze in her tracks when she saw my husband Carl and me walking toward her on a narrow, sandy road in the African bush. She was alone, and terror showed in her face. No wonder! Carl must have looked like a towering white giant to her, and our Great Dane, walking beside us, was enormous.

Carl spoke gently to the frightened child. Immediately, the terror in her eyes changed to wonder and she started walking again. What made the difference? Carl spoke her language. In words she understood, he said to the girl, 'All is well. You are safe.'

Shepherds in the fields that first Christmas night were terrified when they saw angels in the heavens, praising God. But their terror turned to joyful wonder when the messenger of God spoke kindly to them in a language they understood: the language of stables, mangers and babies. Yes, they knew all about barns, feeding troughs and newborn lambs. All was well. They were safe. God came to the shepherds and comes to us in a word we can relate to. Let us hurry, like the shepherds, to worship the Lamb of God.

Prayer: *Thank you, merciful and loving God, for speaking to us in a language we can understand. Help us to proclaim the good news in ways that others, too, can comprehend. In the name of Jesus we pray. Amen*

Thought for the day: God speaks our language.

Deborah Slate Ginder (Virginia, US)

Our Refuge and Strength

Read Psalm 46:1–3

[The Lord] will hide me in his shelter in the day of trouble.
Psalm 27:5 (NRSV)

Eight minutes was the allotted time for two of us to share during one exercise in a devotional-writing workshop. But I alone needed more than eight minutes—not to mention a lot of courage—to share my innermost pain and struggle with a person I had just met. However, the words flowed easily as my partner and I each talked about a recent life challenge.

In our conversation, my pain resonated with my partner's pain. I realised that my pain was no longer as debilitating as when I first experienced it. My partner and I found that we overcame pain not because time healed our wounds but because we sought shelter in God and drew strength from what we believed he can do in our personal circumstances.

Prayers and daily Bible reading comforted and encouraged us to remain firm in our faith. Family, friends and church members prayed for us and with us, and stood beside us in our worst moments of doubt and desperation. God showed us that we were never alone in our struggles.

Prayer: *Almighty God, teach us to turn to you at the first sign of trouble rather than trying to bear our pain alone, for you are our refuge and strength. Amen*

Thought for the day: Pain lessens when we seek God's refuge and strength.

Maritez Cruz (Quezon City, Philippines)

The Power of a Whisper

Read Luke 10:38–42
Be still, and know that I am God; I will be exalted among the nations, I will be exalted in the earth.
Psalm 46:10 (NIV)

It was bedtime, and my daughters needed to go to sleep. Rather than settling down, they were winding up. An earlier game of hide and seek had escalated into a full-blown giggle-fest. When my little girls are playing, I often must whisper to get their attention. Raising my voice doesn't help; they just don't hear it. But whispering causes them to quiet down and focus on what I am saying. Only then can they hear my advice or encouragement.

At times I too get sucked into the distraction of activity—cutting the lawn, driving the children to football practice, nights out with my wife, exercise routines or men's prayer breakfasts. Many of my activities are in themselves commendable, until I notice that the Lord has been trying to get my attention.

Jesus often whispers for us to come and sit at his feet. When we take time to disconnect ourselves from our flurry of daily activities, we can hear God's voice much more clearly.

Prayer: *God of peace, help us to put you first in our lives. Teach us to slow down and allow your voice to nudge our hearts. Amen*

Thought for the day: Slowing down helps us to hear God's voice.

Tez Brooks (Florida, US)

Heart to Keep Trying

Read 1 Thessalonians 5:16–18

Give thanks in all circumstances; for this is God's will for you in Christ Jesus.

1 Thessalonians 5:18 (NIV)

When I began running, the training was hard. Each run felt like an impossible mountain I had to climb. As I forced myself to continue, I found that remembering the blessings in my life helped me. During my run, as I reached the point of wanting to give up, I whispered to God, 'Thank you for legs that work so that I can run. Some people cannot run and wish they could. Thank you for lungs that take in air as I run. Thank you for breath. Some people are fighting for each breath.' Prayer changed my focus and helped me to push through the hardest part of my run.

Similarly, when I face hardships, I sometimes want to stop trying. I want to feel sorry for myself, but doing so often brings me more discouragement and disappointment. I am learning to look for things to be thankful for, even in situations I don't like.

Prayer helps in other areas of my life as well. Remembering the blessings I have is a simple practice, but it accomplishes a mighty change of heart. When I feel discouraged, I remember what God has given me and I find new strength to keep trying. A change of focus creates a change of attitude and motivation.

Prayer: *Loving God, you give us good things. When we are overwhelmed, remind us of all your blessings. Amen*

Thought for the day: Giving thanks to God brings us hope and joy.

Joanne E. Groff (Pennsylvania, US)

Genuine Need, Genuine Gratitude

Read Luke 17:11–19

Don't judge, so that you won't be judged.
Matthew 7:1 (CEB)

During my college training for the ministry, I was appointed to an inner-city church near Sydney. While there we had many callers at the parsonage door looking for a handout. Because my wife and I heard some very tall tales of need, I sometimes viewed these requests with suspicion.

One morning a man called at the door seeking help. I told him that our church was not geared to do much, but if he would walk about 20 minutes up the street a church there was organised to help people in need. He thanked me and left.

Later that day the man came back. When I asked how I could help, he said, ' I have come back to thank you for your help. At the church you sent me to, they gave me food, some better clothing and some money in payment for helping them with some jobs they needed doing.'

I thanked him for coming back and wished him God's blessing. I learned from that encounter not to judge others hastily, as we may never know when someone who asks for our help might have a genuine need.

Prayer: *Dear Lord, help us to be more like Jesus and look for the good in those we meet rather than making hasty judgements. Amen*

Thought for the day: Today I will show God's love to others without hesitation.

Jim MacLean (Queensland, Australia)

Giving to Others

Read Philippians 2:1–4

Do nothing out of selfish ambition or vain conceit.
Philippians 2:3 (NIV)

A few days after Christmas I received an email from one of my favourite shops, announcing a sale. My mind went directly to my bank account balance, to work out what I could afford to spend.

Thoughts of shopping made me remember that only a month before I had shopped for items like clothes, toothpaste and sweets to fill shoeboxes for an organisation that distributes the boxes to poor children living in other countries.

Jesus said that the poor will be with us always (see Mark 14:7), and so we need to care for those around us. The homeless people in my community depend on others for food and shelter, and many times God has prompted me to give to them. I've never missed what I've given, and I've never regretted giving. Now I had a choice to spend money on myself or to use the money to help others. I asked myself two questions I often ask before buying something: do I need it and will I miss it?

Thinking about how a tube of toothpaste or a warm scarf could make a difference in a child's life helped me to decide to use my money to help others. Years ago, I realised that what matters to God is for us to pay attention to the needs of others and give whole-heartedly.

Prayer: *Remind us, dear God, that putting others' needs before our own is a sign of our love for you. Amen*

Thought for the day: I will listen for God's prompting to give whole-heartedly to others.

Judith Williams (Florida, US)

Reflections

Read 1 John 1:3–9

Let your light shine before others, that they may see your good deeds and glorify your Father in heaven.
Matthew 5:16 (NIV)

One of my favourite photographs shows the majestic snow-capped peak of Mount Rainier in Washington State, reflected clearly in the still blue waters of a nearby lake. When I look at the photo, it reminds me that I am called to be a reflection of Christ as I go about my daily routine. My words, my deeds, everything about me can be an example of Christ to those around me.

I often wonder whether my actions reflect Jesus' love as clearly as the calm water reflects Mount Rainier. I doubt it! But neither is the image of Mount Rainier perfectly reflected on the water in the photo. I am not a perfect reflection of Christ, but I find comfort in the knowledge that God doesn't expect me to be perfect but only to be as faithful as I can be. Even with our imperfections, God calls us to be faithful reflections of his love. Who will see Christ through us today?

Prayer: *Dear God, help us to reflect your love so that others see you in all that we say and do. We pray as Jesus taught us, saying, 'Our Father which art in heaven, Hallowed be thy name. Thy kingdom come. Thy will be done in earth, as it is in heaven. Give us this day our daily bread. And forgive us our debts, as we forgive our debtors. And lead us not into temptation, but deliver us from evil: For thine is the kingdom, and the power, and the glory, for ever.'* Amen*

Thought for the day: God does not expect perfection—only faithfulness.

Robert K. Abel (Maryland, US)

Small Group Questions

Wednesday 2 September

1. Have you ever had an experience like the one Veronica writes about in today's meditation? If so, describe that experience. If not, what do you think of Veronica's story?

2. When have you been surprised by someone who met your particular need at just the right time? How did you feel?

3. Do you believe that people can be God's instruments for answering prayers? Why or why not?

4. What helps you to be 'sensitive to the promptings of the Holy Spirit' in your daily life? Are there particular practices or people that help you pay attention to the Spirit?

5. Where in your community do you see people responding to Jesus' teaching to love one another? What are you most impressed by? In what way could you become involved?

Wednesday 9 September

1. When you were learning to pray, did you feel that God expected a certain type or length of prayer? If so, was it easy or difficult to fulfil that expectation?

2. Who taught you to pray? Did he or she teach you a particular prayer? Did you learn to pray at particular times of day? Do you still pray this way?

3. Cliff describes taking short 'intermissions' throughout his day to focus on God. Is this practice something you already do? Is it a practice you would like to adopt?

4. What makes it difficult for you to pray? Are you too busy? Are you angry with God? Do you simply forget? What helps you begin to pray even if it feels difficult?

5. How does your church community teach children and new members to pray? What prayers do you pray together as a congregation? How do these prayers help you in your own prayer life?

Wednesday 16 September

1. Can you relate to Jane's experience of knowing someone so well that you seem to know what the other is thinking? Who is this person for you?

2. How have you developed deep relationships with others? Through conversation? Through shared interests and activities?

3. Do you think this kind of relationship is something that only happens with people who already think like you, or do you think this kind of relationship can develop with anyone if you try hard enough? Why?

4. Jesus prays for his disciples to be unified as he and God are one— 'I in them and you in me' (John 17:22, NIV). What does this mean to you? What would it be like to be one with God? To be 'brought to complete unity' with God?

5. What practices, prayers or people help you to feel close to God? How do you work toward having a closer relationship with God?

Wednesday 23 September

1. Recall a time you felt exhausted and unprepared for your day. What led to these feelings? How did you handle them? How was God present for you during that time?

2. Whom do you take care of? Do you ever find yourself feeling burdened or burned out by caring for these people? What helps you to rest and renew your energy?

3. Who has cared for you when you have needed care? Did you ask for their care? Do they ever surprise you by caring for you in unexpected ways? How do you show your appreciation for the people who care for you?

4. How does your faith help to renew and refresh you when you feel exhausted or burdened? What prayers or spiritual practices help you to reconnect with God and find strength?

5. The story of Elijah reminds us that God appears in mysterious and unexpected ways. How does your church help people to recognise God even when he appears in unexpected places?

Wednesday 30 September

1. When have you helped with building or transforming a home? What did you like about that work? What aspects did you find difficult? How did you feel when the work was complete?

2. John writes in today's meditation, 'I am a work in progress, being transformed day by day by a loving God.' Do you agree with John? How do you know this to be true in your own life? Give an example.

3. What Bible passages do you turn to when you need to be reminded of thoughts, actions or attitudes that bring glory to God? Have you memorised particular verses that help you focus on giving glory to God?

4. What habits or attitudes sometimes prevent you from sharing God's transforming love with others?

5. In what ways are you working with God to transform your life? What spiritual practices, volunteer opportunities or work help you to continue the transforming work God has begun in you?

Wednesday 7 October

1. Have you or has someone you care about suffered from depression or addiction? Describe that experience.

2. When you are in despair, what do you do? Whom do you turn to for help? Do you cry out to God? What do you pray?

3. Recall a time when God answered your prayer. What was your prayer? How did God answer it? Was the answer what you expected? How did this answer to prayer comfort or surprise you?

4. How have your experiences of trouble or despair challenged or encouraged you to support others? How have you connected with or supported others in their times of despair?

5. What programmes, groups or ministries does your church offer to help those who are struggling with issues of addiction or mental health? What other opportunities might there be to help these people?

Wednesday 14 October

1. Do you have any personal experience with people in prison or individuals who are on the margins of society? Describe your experience.

2. Recall a conversation you have had about forgiveness. Were you the person needing reassurance of forgiveness or the one assuring someone else of being forgiven?

3. How easy or difficult is it for you to forgive yourself? Is belief in God's forgiveness simple or challenging for you?

4. Lyle writes that 'God's love is our refuge in all times.' How has this been true in your life? Describe how it feels to take refuge in God's love. What do you do to remind yourself of God's unconditional love?

5. How does your church assure people of forgiveness? What acts of hospitality and welcome help non-members of your church to know that God loves them? What other ways can you imagine for your church to assure people that God forgives and loves them?

Wednesday 21 October

1. Describe your favourite season of the year. What are your favourite sights, sounds, smells, temperatures and flavours during this time of year? How do you celebrate or enjoy spending time during this season?

2. Where do you go to spend time reading the Bible? Is this a private act for you? Is reading the Bible a regular part of your day?

3. How do you make time for God during your daily life? Can you take breaks at work to pray or study scripture? If so, do you?

4. Do you live in a place where people practise their faith openly in public places? Can you relate to Wilma's experience of observing others studying scripture or otherwise spending time with God? Is this something you would like to do or wish was possible in your community?

5. How do you share your faith with others? What do you want to do to model a life of faith for others who might be observing you?

Wednesday 28 October

1. What do you think of Sharamae's story? Does carrying a gratitude stone seem like a good idea to you?

2. Recall a time when you were impatient or frustrated. Describe the situation. What did you do? Did you pray or complain to God—or something else?

3. How easy or difficult is it for you to 'give thanks in every situation' (1 Thessalonians 5:18, CEB)? Whom do you know who seems to give thanks always? What do you admire about this person or these people? How do they remain grateful despite challenging circumstances?

4. How do you remember to give thanks to God in your daily life? What spiritual practices help you to show gratitude?

5. In what ways can you help to remind others to be grateful? How can you model giving thanks to God for your family, friends and community? What practice will help you turn complaints into words of thanks?

Wednesday 4 November

1. Recall a time when you prayed for something specific. What did you pray for? Was your prayer answered in the way you expected it would be?

2. How do you deal with prayers that do not seem to be answered in the way you hoped for? What do you do when it seems as if your prayer is not being answered? What helps you to keep praying through these times?

3. Are you more comfortable praying for specific issues, people and problems, or do you prefer to pray in more general ways? Why are you more comfortable praying in this way?

4. What do you think of Joan's practice of praying more specifically? How might you apply this practice to your life? What specific prayer will you offer up today?

5. Describe how you pray best. Are you alone? With a trusted group or partner? Do you pray prayers that are already written out? What new way of praying would you like to try or begin including in your regular routine?

Wednesday 11 November

1. Can you identify with Avon's story? When have you experienced disappointment, a dream that you could not fulfil or a betrayal by a friend? How did you feel? What did you do?

2. When you experience disappointment or bitterness, what helps you to heal and move forward? Who has modelled this healing or helped you to find peace during these times?

3. When have you prayed for God to change you? What change did you seek? How did praying help you at that time? How did God help you to make a change?

4. When have you had difficulty forgiving someone? What makes forgiveness difficult? How do you work through the difficulty and seek to forgive others?

5. What studies, sermons or Bible readings have helped to shape your understanding of forgiveness? How has your church helped to teach you about forgiveness?

Wednesday 18 November

1. What was your first reaction to Teresa's meditation? What surprised you? Where did you find encouragement and joy in this story? What made you uncomfortable?

2. Have you ever been the recipient of unexpected hospitality? Describe that experience. What did it feel like to be noticed, helped or welcomed?

3. How have your own experiences of receiving hospitality shaped or changed your practice of extending hospitality? How do you try to welcome strangers, help neighbours and show kindness to the people around you in your daily life?

4. What does hospitality mean to you? Who has modelled hospitality for you in your life? What books, people or scripture passages have helped you to think about hospitality in new ways?

5. What ministries or missions does your church lead or participate in that offer hospitality to your community? In what other ways might your church extend hospitality to others?

Wednesday 25 November

1. Have you or has someone you know experienced something like the grief Chris describes in her meditation? How did your experience differ from Chris's? How was it similar?

2. How did family, friends or church members reach out to you in your time of grief? What gestures were the most helpful? Why?

3. How have you supported others in times of sorrow? How do you express your sympathy and try to share God's love and peace at those times? How has your support been received by those who are grieving?

4. Chris describes her struggle with Paul's instruction to 'Rejoice in the Lord always.' When has this been difficult for you? In that time, did you try to find ways to rejoice? Why or why not? If not, what did you do instead? Was it helpful?

5. How does your church support people who are grieving? How could you do this better?

Wednesday 2 December

1. Do you have a regular prayer practice? Do you intentionally pray for others? How do you keep track of the people you are praying for? Do you belong to a prayer group?

2. Is prayer an important part of your daily life? Have you ever felt too busy to pray? What did you do? How did you feel?

3. Who is your prayer role model? What do you admire about that person's prayer practice? What can you learn from the way that person incorporates prayer into his or her life?

4. Recall a time when someone told you they were praying for you. What did this mean to you? How did that knowledge make you feel? Had you asked for prayer?

5. When you are overwhelmed or discouraged, what helps you to keep praying? Who do you turn to for encouragement?

Wednesday 9 December

1. Do you and your friends or family have particular traditions at Christmas time? How do your traditions help you to focus on the meaning of Christmas, and Christ's coming into the world?

2. Who helps you to pay attention to your spiritual life? How does this person help you grow spiritually? What do you appreciate most about this person?

3. How is your spiritual life? What practices, reading or fellowship help you to focus on your faith?

4. What areas of your spiritual life would you like to give more time and attention? How will you focus on these areas in the coming year?

5. How does your church help you to grow spiritually? What parts of worship, community life and teaching help you most in your spiritual life?

Wednesday 16 December

1. Brian describes his personal devotional practice during the Christmas season. Does your devotional practice change during Advent and Christmas? What changes? Are you more or less attentive to your devotional time during this season?

2. What helps you to focus on the meaning of Advent and Christmas? What tools, practices or traditions are most helpful to you during Advent?

3. What distracts you from your faith practices during this season? How do you deal with these distractions?

4. What qualities do you reflect to those you meet each day? What do you hope to reflect to the world this Advent season?

5. How are you reflecting love and compassion to others? How does your church or community make this easy or difficult? What ministries or opportunities are most helpful in allowing you to share love and compassion?

Wednesday 23 December

1. Can you relate to Tim's story? In your experience were you the giver or the receiver of the unexpected gift? How did that experience make you feel?

2. Are you more comfortable giving or receiving gifts? Who taught you to be a generous giver? Who showed you how to be a gracious receiver?

3. Why do you think we feel we must give gifts to those who give to us? Do you think receiving a gift sincerely and graciously can be enough of a gift? Why or why not?

4. How does the practice of giving gifts relate to the meaning of Christmas for you?

5. Have you ever felt that you needed to repay God for the gift of grace? What did you do in an effort to repay God? Do you still feel this way? How have you learned to accept God's love and grace?

Wednesday 30 December

1. What was your reaction to Judith's story? Have you ever been in a similar situation? What decision did you make? How did you feel about your decision?

2. Who taught you about money as a child? What were you taught to do with your money? Save it? Spend it? Give it away? Invest it? How has your use of money changed during your life? What caused this change?

3. What charities, causes or ministries do you most often donate to? Why do you choose to give to these in particular?

4. How does your church model good stewardship? How is money used in your congregation? Does the way money is used reflect the beliefs of your church?

5. Besides money, how do you give of yourself for others? In what ways would you like to be more generous in the coming year? How will you work toward this goal?

Comings and Goings

Retracing the Christmas story through place and time

Gordon Giles

Life involves many 'comings and goings' as we make our way along the path of faith day by day, guided by God's Holy Spirit. This book of readings for Advent and Christmas invites us to make a journey through time, from the end to the very beginning of all things. The daily reflections work backwards from the traditional Advent focus of the 'Four Last Things'—death, judgement, heaven and hell—via Jesus' life, death and resurrection, to come at last to the incarnation and the events commemorated at Christmas itself. In the following days, the focus turns to Christ as the Word of God, present at the dawn of creation. Along the way, we 'visit' some of the actual Holy Land sites associated with Gospel events, drawing new insights from the familiar stories.

ISBN 978 0 85746 376 0   £7.99

To order a copy of this book, please turn to the order form on page 159.

The Word was God

Short reflections for Advent

Andy John

Here is a gentle way of walking through the busy days leading up to Christmas.

Here is encouragement to slow down and savour the words of one of the best-loved of seasonal Bible readings.

Here is refreshment for heart and soul as well as inspiration for sharing the good news of Jesus' birth with others.

ISBN 978 0 85746 424 8   £6.99

To order a copy of this book, please turn to the order form on page 159.

A Christian Guide to Environmental Issues

Martin and Margot Hodson

Environmental sustainability is a major issue in society today. While Christian response was generally slow in the 1980s and '90s, concern has grown rapidly in the 21st century across the church. In this book, two environmental experts consider eight of the key contemporary issues, offering eco-tips to enable practice response, as well as Bible-based reflections to deepen understanding. Among the issues covered are climate change, food, biodiversity and population—and the relationship between environmental problems and issues relating to world development.

ISBN 978 0 85746 383 8   £9.99
To order a copy of this book, please turn to the order form on page 159.

The No-Rehearsal Nativity

A church nativity resource with a difference

Janine Gillion

Bring everyone together in a no-fuss, pure enjoyment retelling of the Christmas story!

The No-Rehearsal Nativity makes it possible for churches to put on a nativity play that families in their congregation and local community can simply join in with on the day. Ideal for service leaders who lack the time or confidence to organise a rehearsed nativity play, it also provides a way to involve families who do not normally attend church or are visiting over Christmas.

Includes full script, advice on preparation, publicity and staging, and options to set the play within a Christingle or crib service. A 'no-sew nativity' appendix provides instructions and templates for making simple costumes on a budget.

ISBN 978 0 85746 366 1   £8.99
To order a copy of this book, please turn to the order form on page 159.

How to encourage Bible reading in your church

BRF has been helping individuals connect with the Bible for over 90 years. We want to support churches as they seek to encourage church members into regular Bible reading.

Order a Bible reading resources pack
This pack is designed to give your church the tools to publicise our Bible reading notes. It includes:

- Sample Bible reading notes for your congregation to try.
- Publicity resources, including a poster.
- A church magazine feature about Bible reading notes.

The pack is free, but we welcome a £5 donation to cover the cost of postage. If you require a pack to be sent outside the UK or require a specific number of sample Bible reading notes, please contact us for postage costs. More information about what the current pack contains is available on our website.

How to order and find out more
- Visit **www.biblereadingnotes.org.uk/for-churches/**
- Telephone BRF on 01865 319700 between 9.15 am and 5.30 pm.
- Write to us at BRF, 15 The Chambers, Vineyard, Abingdon, OX14 3FE.

Keep informed about our latest initiatives
We are continuing to develop resources to help churches encourage people into regular Bible reading, wherever they are on their journey. Join our email list at **www.biblereadingnotes.org.uk/helpingchurches/** to stay informed about the latest initiatives that your church could benefit from.

Introduce a friend to our notes
We can send information about our notes and current prices for you to pass on. Please contact us.

Subscriptions

The Upper Room is published in January, May and September.

Individual subscriptions

The subscription rate for orders for 4 or fewer copies includes postage and packing: THE UPPER ROOM annual individual subscription   £16.20

Church subscriptions

Orders for 5 copies or more, sent to ONE address, are post free:
THE UPPER ROOM annual church subscription   £12.75

Please do not send payment with order for a church subscription. We will send an invoice with your first order.

Please note that the annual billing period for church subscriptions runs from 1 May to 30 April.

Copies of the notes may also be obtained from Christian bookshops.

Single copies of *The Upper Room* will cost £4.25. Prices valid until 30 April 2016.

Giant print version

The Upper Room is available in giant print for the visually impaired, from:

Torch Trust for the Blind
Torch House
Torch Way,
Northampton Road
Market Harborough
LE16 9HL

Tel: 01858 438260
www.torchtrust.org

Individual Subscriptions

☐ I would like to take out a subscription myself (complete your name and address details only once)

☐ I would like to give a gift subscription (please complete both name and address sections below)

Your name...

Your addre ....

....Postcode......................................

Your telephone number..

Gift subscription name..

Gift subscription address..

....Postcode......................................

Gift message (20 words max)..

....

Please send *The Upper Room* beginning with the January 2016 / May 2016 / September 2016 issue: (delete as applicable)

THE UPPER ROOM ☐ £16.20

Please complete the payment details below and send, with appropriate payment, to: BRF, 15 The Chambers, Vineyard, Abingdon OX14 3FE

Total enclosed £.......... (cheques should be made payable to 'BRF')

Payment by ☐ cheque ☐ postal order ☐ Visa ☐ Mastercard ☐ Switch

Card no: ☐☐☐☐☐☐☐☐☐☐☐☐☐☐☐☐☐☐☐☐☐☐☐☐

Expires: ☐☐☐☐   Security code: ☐☐☐

Issue no (Switch): ☐☐☐☐

Signature (essential if paying by credit/Switch card) ....

☐ Please do not send me further information about BRF publications

☐ Please send me a Bible reading resources pack to encourage Bible reading in my church

BRF is a Registered Charity

Church Subscriptions

☐ Please send me ... copies of *The Upper Room* January 2016 / May 2016 / September 2016 issue (delete as applicable)

Name...

Address ....

....Postcode...

Telephone ....

Email...

Please send this completed form to:
BRF, 15 The Chambers, Vineyard, Abingdon OX14 3FE

Please do not send payment with this order. We will send an invoice with your first order.

Christian bookshops: All good Christian bookshops stock BRF publications. For your nearest stockist, please contact BRF.

Telephone: The BRF office is open between 09.15 and 17.30. To place your order, telephone 01865 319700; fax 01865 319701.

Web: Visit www.brf.org.uk

☐ Please send me a Bible reading resources pack to encourage Bible reading in my church

BRF is a Registered Charity

ORDERFORM

REF	TITLE	PRICE	QTY	TOTAL
376 0	Comings and Goings	£7.99		
424 8	The Word was God	£6.99		
383 8	Christian Guide Environmental Issues	£9.99		
366 1	No-Rehearsal Nativity	£8.99		
		Postage and packing		
		Donation		
		TOTAL		

POSTAGE AND PACKING CHARGES				
Order value	UK	Europe	Economy (Surface)	Standard (Air)
Under £7.00	£1.25	£3.00	£3.50	£5.50
£7.00–£29.99	£2.25	£5.50	£6.50	£10.00
£30.00 and over	free	prices on request		

Name _____ Account Number _____

Address _____

_____ Postcode _____

Telephone Number_____

Email _____

Payment by: ❏ Cheque ❏ Mastercard ❏ Visa ❏ Postal Order ❏ Maestro

Card no ⬜⬜⬜⬜ ⬜⬜⬜⬜ ⬜⬜⬜⬜ ⬜⬜⬜⬜ ⬜⬜⬜

Valid from ⬜⬜⬜⬜ Expires ⬜⬜⬜⬜ Issue no. ⬜⬜

Security code* ⬜⬜⬜ *Last 3 digits on the reverse of the card. ESSENTIAL IN ORDER TO PROCESS YOUR ORDER   Shaded boxes for Maestro use only

Signature _____ Date _____

All orders must be accompanied by the appropriate payment.

Please send your completed order form to:
BRF, 15 The Chambers, Vineyard, Abingdon OX14 3FE
Tel. 01865 319700 / Fax. 01865 319701 Email: enquiries@brf.org.uk

❏ Please send me further information about BRF publications.

Available from your local Christian bookshop.   BRF is a Registered Charity

About
brf:

BRF is a registered charity and also a limited company, and has been in existence since 1922. Through all that we do—producing resources, providing training, working face-to-face with adults and children, and via the web—we work to resource individuals and church communities in their Christian discipleship through the Bible, prayer and worship.

Our Barnabas children's team works with primary schools and churches to help children under 11, and the adults who work with them, to explore Christianity creatively and to bring the Bible alive.

To find out more about BRF and its core activities and ministries, visit:

www.brf.org.uk
www.brfonline.org.uk
www.biblereadingnotes.org.uk
www.barnabasinschools.org.uk
www.barnabasinchurches.org.uk
www.faithinhomes.org.uk
www.messychurch.org.uk

If you have any questions about BRF and our work, please email us at

enquiries@brf.org.uk